AF413772

THREE GRAND REBELLIONS

Three Grand Rebellions

A Biblical Love Story of Redemption, The Undoing of Eden, Nephilim, and Babel's Fall

Pete Robertson

Set Free Press

Contents

Introduction

Before you Begin

In the intricate tapestry of existence, woven within the threads of history and eternity, lies a thin line, often unseen, but holding fast the narrative of the cosmos. "Three Grand Rebellions: A Bible Love Story of redemption & the Undoing of Eden, Nephilim, and Babel's Fall" is an invitation to embark on a profound journey, a quest to illuminate the subtle and profound intricacies of divine design that have too often lain concealed in the shadows of our understanding.

Through the pages of this book, we will traverse ancient paths and peer into the alcoves of history, searching for the fingerprints of the Almighty in the unfolding of time. We will seek the whispers of truth that have echoed down through the ages, truths that have shaped kings and kingdoms, prophets and the poor, and ultimately, the heart of every person who has ever drawn breath.

It is a journey that demands courage, for to step out of the shadows is to challenge the obscurity that cloaks complacency. With each chapter, we draw back veils that might have obscured our sight, revealing a landscape rich with intention and brimming with promise.

"Three Grand Rebellions" is not just a scholarly exposition; it is an odyssey that bridges the realms of the theological and the personal. It beckons you to discover the unbroken thread that weaves through scripture, history, and your own life story—a thread that leads to a deeper understanding of the majestic blueprint devised by the Master Weaver.

As we venture forth, leaving behind the dimly lit corridors of conjecture and stepping into the radiance of revelation. Together, we will uncover the hidden threads of God's grand plan and, in doing so, find that what once might have seemed mere shadow play is, in fact, a masterclass in luminous truth.

DISCIPLESHIP CINEMATIC TRANSFORMATION

I envision this book as a richly cinematic script experience, unfolding like an epic movie before your eyes. Within its pages, you'll find yourself cast in the leading role, immersed firsthand in a grand and intricately crafted narrative tapestry.

Meanwhile, I will serve as both guide and narrator, delicately peeling back the layers of the tale to reveal the deeper meanings and connections that you, the principal character, are experiencing. Together, we'll navigate the delicate interplay between your direct encounters and the broader, insightful commentary that provides context to your adventure.

I will constantly share throughout the book about how incredibly good God is. It is my sincere hope that each and every reader will develop a deep desire to know Him on a profound level.

The inspiration for writing this book stems from an overflow of my personal discipleship experiences with God's teachings in His word. I view this book as a powerful tool for discipleship, as reading it will ignite a hunger in your mind to explore the depths of God's truth further.

On a personal note, Discipleship holds a place of great significance in my life, a theme that will echo across the subsequent pages. A disciple is one who follows Jesus with discipline, continuously striving to embody His teachings and extend this pursuit by guiding others to do the same.

At Natural Discipleship, the organization with which I am affiliated, our core commitment lies in cultivating heartfelt dialogues and encouraging spiritual development. We form an international collective of pastors, leaders, and students, all united by our unwavering belief in the profound impact of transformative conversations.

By equipping individuals with the necessary training tools, we actively strive to fulfill the great commission. Our approach enables disciples to not only follow Christ but also be transformed by Him and join Him in His mission.

Knowing God personally and aiding others in their journey to know Him should be at the core of our life's purpose.

In Matthew 4:19, Jesus instructs His disciples to leave their fishing business and devote themselves to building God's kingdom. While they may still maintain their livelihood through fishing, their primary focus becomes understanding the Father and sharing His truth with others.

In the initial two chapters, I'll lay the foundation, meticulously constructing the framework of the grand plan that will eventually reverse the Three Grand Rebellions. This will serve as the cornerstone of our narrative journey. Upon this foundation, we will then transition smoothly into the science fiction elements of the book, steering you through a riveting interpretation that converges with the Three Grand Rebellions chronicled in the Bible.

This pathway ultimately steers us toward the pivotal figure of Jesus. As we look deeper, I will unravel the profound implications of His birth, death, and resurrection, revelations that transcend the traditional teachings of Sunday School, offering a more expansive and awe-inspiring perspective of His role in the cosmos.

My hope is you find this book to be a blessing, I encourage you to share it with someone else and continue to strive towards finishing the race of faith strongly. Let's get started with Chapter 1 The Grand Narrative unfolds.

Chapter 1

The Grand Narrative Unfolds

Picture yourself as the main character in an epic romance sci-fi adventure, where the entangling threads of passion and interstellar intrigue are as unyielding as the expanse of space itself. Here, you are the heart and soul of a narrative that thrives on the complexities of love set against a canvas of cosmic wonders, crafting a story where emotions run as deep as the mysteries of the universe that you're destined to explore.

This journey will transport you back in time and then propel you into the future. As you read through it, imagine the credits roll, the music swells, and the camera zooms in on you in a world brimming with questions and yearning for answers.

Around you, the shadows of biblical history and mystery dance together, forming patterns that you've long desired to decipher. You sense that you're on the cusp of an understanding that bridges time, an unveiling of divine strategy that's about to unfold before you.

In your quest for truth, you open the sacred pages of the Bible. You recall the love encapsulated in the greatest commandment shared by Jesus in Matthew 22:37, where He instructs us to "Love the Lord your God with all your heart and with all your soul and with all your mind."

This profound directive sets the scene for the journey you're embarking upon—a journey that shapes the narrative of your life. Love anchors every scene, every act, every dialog, guiding you to live out the sequel "Love your neighbor as yourself."

These are the themes that resound throughout this epic romance sci-fi adventure, where the desire for closeness with the Creator influences every relationship, every encounter you experience.

At its core, the Bible is often perceived as a grand narrative of love and redemption, where divine affection and the restoration of a fractured relationship between God and humanity take center stage.

As the main character in this tale, you come to realize the necessity of complete surrender to the author of existence. Amid scenes of prayer, worship, and the exploration of His word, you align yourself with His presence. This intimate connection with God, reminiscent of the psalmist's meditations, seasons every aspect of your life.

Now, as you embark on your calling, you find yourself equipped, as 1 Peter 3:15 reveals, to *"give an answer to everyone who asks you to give the reason for the hope that you have."* In your study and research, in the outpouring of divine revelation, joy and satisfaction fill you, illuminating the storyline of your days.

Deeper Knowledge of God

This movie of life you're living showcases the transformative power of intimacy with the Father. It is a testament to the impact one can make when one sees through the compassionate lens of Jesus. The evidence is clear—genuine affection for people doesn't spring from the natural well of human behavior; it is a heaven-sent miracle, born of time spent in the presence of God.

As scenes of the movie play out, you, the main character, share with the audience—the readers of this book—an offer to journey together into a deeper knowledge of God.

Big Idea of the book

As we transition from the experiences you will encounter as the main character, I, the narrator, will provide personal insights.

Throughout the Bible, there is a single thread that intertwines every narrative, and this book aims to unravel its significance. As you look into its pages, you will gain a profound clarity of this thread, while simultaneously uncovering God's grand plan that has been in motion since the beginning of time.

It is true that the Old Testament can sometimes appear perplexing, with its seemingly otherworldly verses discussing gods beyond mere idols and angels engaging in relationships with humans.

However, I will bring to light how these elements are intricately connected to the overarching thread, thereby enabling you to grasp a deeper understanding of the one true Creator God, Yahweh. Ultimately, this journey will nurture a greater love for God, propelling you toward fulfilling your unique purpose and divine calling.

We will also explore how this thread extends into the New Testament, illuminating the profound impact of Jesus' birth, death, burial, and resurrection. Through His redemptive work, Jesus not only saved us from our sins but also offered clarity regarding our existence and restored our fellowship with the divine spiritual world.

The entire Bible has one ultimate focus: leading people to Jesus, the savior who redeems and saves humanity from eternal separation from God. Redemption, defined as being saved from sin, error, or evil, is the crux of Jesus's mission. His purpose was to restore the possibility for all of humanity, not just the Israelites, to have fellowship with a holy God.

Jesus' Ministry Addressed More Than Just Adam's Sin

I will reveal that Jesus's earthly ministry went beyond addressing Adam's sin. He also addressed the divine rebellion in Genesis 6:1-4 and the rebellion at the Tower of Babel in Genesis 11. In this context, I will piece together a mosaic of truths that showcase how Christ's obedience achieved even more than we had previously understood.

Over the years, I have encountered a common question: why did God reject the world and choose only the Jewish nation for salvation? Few have pondered the idea of God's rejection, but when He set apart Israel for Himself, that is precisely what occurred.

The Jewish nation emerged as a direct consequence of the sin committed at the Tower of Babel. I will emphasize the significance of God's plan in turning His back on the world while allowing them to worship other gods, shedding light on His divine purpose.

Another question I aim to address is the controversial topic of angels having relationships with humans, as mentioned in Genesis 6:1-4. This notion may resemble Greek or Roman mythology, but according to the Bible, it did happen.

The consequence of this disobedience was God's decision to flood the earth and start anew. I perceive God's response to this act of divine disobedience in the coming of Jesus. His birth, death, burial, and resurrection all serve as a means to address this sin, providing clarity to God's grand plan.

As we journey through these revelations, may you gain a deeper understanding of how Jesus's redemption transcends what we may previously comprehend.

Is Hercules a Real Character?

This is a funny question I have gotten before that really has little significance to this book but I would like to answer it. Could Hercules who was known to be half man and half god be a real-life character? I think it could be a reference to Gen 6:1-4 and the Nephilim (Hero Giants). For many that do not know Hercules is believed to be the son of Zeus, king of the gods, and the mortal woman Alcmene.

Zeus, who was always chasing one woman or another, took on the form of Alcmene's husband, Amphitryon, and visited Alcmene one night in her bed, and so Hercules was born a demi-god with incredible strength and stamina. I think a lot of Greek/Roman mythology comes from what happened after the Tower of Babel. I do not see these questions as significant in God's grand plan, I just think it's a fun question to ponder.

Did Israel Believe in More Than One God?

One topic that has intrigued many over the course of history is whether or not the Jewish people believed in multiple gods. It is true that they acknowledged the existence of other divine beings that held control, perhaps even being perceived as gods. However, at their core, they firmly believed in one true living creator God, Yahweh. In the upcoming pages, I will look into this belief and how it provides us with a clearer understanding of God's grand plan.

Now, if the Jewish people acknowledged the presence of other controlling beings that could be seen as gods, one might ask if Christians also believe in multiple gods. To unravel this question, we must examine the Jewish nation's interpretation of their writings within the appropriate context.

From this perspective, we begin to unveil the mysteries of the Godhead, which were revealed to His apostles. This understanding reveals that God is one, comprised of three distinct persons: the Father, the Son, and the Holy Spirit. Throughout the Bible, there are references to other god-like entities, and I will explore how this ties into God's over-arching plan when viewed in the proper context.

By exploring these aspects, we will gain a comprehensive perspective on the Jewish belief system and how it aligns with the understanding of the Godhead in Christian the-ology. This deeper comprehension will shed light on the underlying coherence of God's grand plan.

God's Ultimate Goal for Us

Ultimately, God desires for us to have an intimate knowl-edge of Him. He longs for us to understand His thoughts, His decision-making process, and the reasons behind His actions. While our daily quiet time with Him and reading His Word contribute to this pursuit, it is crucial that we go beyond surface-level reading.

We must study the Bible with intention and dig into its depths, allowing our relationship with Jesus to mirror the unity between Him and the Father. This book serves as a valuable companion to the Bible, unveiling possibly overlooked verses that hold significant meaning. By exploring its pages, you will gain increased clarity and a deeper understanding of the Bible in a context that few have ever seen before.

My sincerest hope is that as you engage with these forthcoming chapters, your desire to dig deeper and truly know Jesus will be stirred within you. He is profoundly good, unfailingly faithful, and deserving of our heartfelt praise. May your time spent reading this book inspire a thirst for a more profound and intimate relationship with Jesus than you have ever experienced before.

Writing this book has made me realize that the more I know about God and His character the more happier and joy-filled I become.

The overflow of my time with God results in my love for His people, I begin to see people as Jesus sees them. It truly is a miracle when I show compassion to others; when I extend grace and do my best to elevate others above myself. There is no way this happens naturally in my life without intimacy with the Father.

In the following chapter, we will look deeper into the tapestry of God's divine love story, while continuing to unravel the intricate details of the three grand rebellions.

Chapter 2

Interwoven Destinies: The Epic Beyond Easter

Most love stories seem to share a familiar script: a boy meets a girl, they kindle a friendship, which blossoms into love. Their journey together commences—a shared life, raising children, aiming for that elusive 'happily ever after.' Of course, the path is sprinkled with drama, crafting a narrative tapestry of their shared experiences.

We consume endless books and films portraying these narratives. Some capture our imagination more than others, yet they follow a recognizable pattern. A promising start, an ensuing struggle, and then emerges a hero, who may or may not resolve the crisis, writing the rest as history.

I confess I have a soft spot for a gripping book or a stirring romance film, though I have an innate preference for action. Nevertheless, watching a romantic film has become an activity that brings joy to my wife, and I've learned to appreciate them alongside her.

Once, at a men's bible study, when asked about my favorite movie, I declared 'The Notebook' with assertive pride, eliciting laughter and light-hearted jests that linger to this day.

But why 'The Notebook'? It resonates with the story my wife and I share. This is the magic of movies—they draw us into their drama, offering a window into another life, and sometimes, if we're lucky, they mirror our own, letting us live vicariously through their tales.

In recent times, the silver screen has been awash with Sci-Fi and superhero epics. They whisk our imaginations away to realms of wonder, presenting us with feats and worlds so extraordinary that they defy our reality.

Consider Thor, an otherworldly god descending to Earth with his formidable powers – we inherently know such tales are fabrications, mere cinema magic. But what if I told you there's a kernel of truth in these stories? You might think I'm tipping into madness, but bear with me.

I invite you on a voyage through a narrative that encapsulates all the elements of the most enthralling film you've ever encountered. It's a love story infused with drama, action, Sci-Fi, and superhuman characters – and astonishingly, it's based on truth.

By the time you turn the final page of this book, I am confident your perspective will be profoundly altered. I even harbor hopes that someday this tale will leap from these pages to the motion picture screen, crafted by the skilled hands of filmmakers.

The Bible has often been seen as a difficult book; its messages are shrouded in mystery to the uninitiated. Indeed, without context, its content can seem utterly confounding. As mentioned before, this book aims to latch onto a thread woven through the entirety of Scripture, granting clarity to its overarching message.

As you continue reading the upcoming chapters, you will assume the role of the main character in an epic cinematic story. Your journey will take you through a variety of interconnected parts that come together in a magnificent grand finale. You will witness our hero, quite expectedly, is Jesus; and our villain, the shadowy legions of a demonic underworld.

3 Grand Rebellions

As mentioned in the introduction chapter there's more to Jesus's mission on Earth than what's typically relayed in Sunday school teachings. Hence the title of this book: "Three Grand Rebellions"

Many of us recognize the profound significance of Easter's Holy Week as the time marking Jesus's life, death, and resurrection. We've been taught, following John 3:16, that by repenting and believing in Jesus as our Lord and Savior, we receive forgiveness and the promise of eternal life. This is, without a doubt, the most loving joyous news—the assurance of salvation. However, have you ever wondered whether there's more to this narrative?

To be clear, I'm not suggesting there are additional steps for salvation; belief in Jesus promises complete forgiveness of sins—past, present, and future. However, upon extensively studying this subject, I have come to realize that Jesus' birth, death, and resurrection were not only meant to redeem humanity from sin caused by Adam's transgression alone.

There is a deeper aspect of this narrative that involves God dealing with the Three Grand Rebellions that include the divine. My conviction is that the story is far richer and in this epic tale—of which you are a participant—we'll dig deep into this grand plan.

Let's journey to a time even before the dawn of creation. Did you know there's a verse in Job hinting at pre-creation events? As we unravel our divine love story, some aspects might seem as fantastical as a Sci-Fi plot—a notion that might prompt you to verify the verses I'll introduce, ensuring I haven't veered into the realm of fantasy. But, to fully understand these rebellions, we must look at hard-to-understand verses in the Bible.

We will study texts that discuss how angels, known as the 'Watchers,' created giants called the 'Nephilim' by interacting with humans. While interpretations may differ, it is clear that the Watchers are of higher status than ordinary angels and are distinct from humans, residing in a celestial realm. Apart from the sin of Adam and Eve, which was the first rebellion, this incident represents the second major rebellion. Furthermore, we will examine the shift that took place at the Tower of Babel, symbolizing the third major rebellion.

Our Main Characters

For many years, I overlooked the nuanced context sprinkled throughout the Bible. It was only when I started diving into the verses that often go unnoticed that I began to uncover the remarkable plan God has been orchestrating from the outset.

The revelations that await in the pages ahead have been transformative for me, illuminating the depth of God's love. This is an adventurous sci-fi love story of epic proportions, with a cast featuring you as the witnessing character, me the narrator, God (Yahweh), Jesus, angels, humanity, and other celestial beings (gods-Elohim) beyond our understanding.

Every Great Love Story Weaves Through

Challenges, Drama and Conflicts

As with any love story, drama is inevitable, and missteps occur between partners. I'm far from flawless; I've made mistakes that have pained my wife. A candid examination of our relationship through the years would reveal the emotional scars I've inflicted. A skilled storyteller would look deeper into those hurts and their impact on our relationship.

They would detail how those injuries have molded our relationship, altering my wife's perception of me from the idealistic days of our wedding. The storyline would unravel how a hardened shell of bitterness has developed, evident in the edge of her voice and the guarded walls she erects, hesitating to share openly for fear of my reaction.

It's clear that a single grave error can start the fabric of trust to fray, and in my story, there was certainly more than one.

The undeniable truth is that unresolved wounds can erode a relationship over time, leading from mere strain to outright deterioration. My own marriage needed mending, and it was through the healing and redemptive power of Jesus that we found restoration to the joy and closeness we once knew.

The narrative thread we'll trace in the Bible echoes the story of my marriage. I've identified three significant rebellions against God that, unless properly addressed by Jesus, would have threatened to disrupt our intimacy and communion with Him.

Yet, the distinction between God and me is stark; I am flawed, but He is the epitome of holiness. God, unlike humans, harbors no bitterness and does not need defenses. His response is one of perfect, righteous love, and He recognizes the necessity for reconciliation to restore fellowship.

His divine plan is not only to mend but to renew all relationships with Him and reinstitute harmony within His entire creation.

So, are you prepared to observe from an unseen vantage point, to adopt a fresh angle on familiar tales? Our next chapter inaugurates with a scene unlike any other—a divine council, with gods conversing upon thrones, deliberating over the fate of the world.

We'll be privy to the unseen mechanics of the universe, gaining insight into the architect behind the grand plan. As I mentioned, this is not fiction; its truth contextualized, and as you absorb the evidence, your comprehension of God's love will deepen.

I recall that moment in 'Rocky IV' when Rocky is bubbling with anticipation to give Adrian a robot bearing her anniversary gift. His childlike excitement is noticeable; and now, with this book in your hands, I share a similar excitement. I'm eager for you to experience how God's touch through these words will transform your life.

Chapter 3

The Heavenly Hierarchy

Before we begin to paint this picture and lay out this chapter, I want to make sure that everyone knows and understands I am a traditional Trinitarian and affirm the deity of Christ. I know for many of us, these scenes might be unfamiliar, and since this is a true story you might feel like I am making this stuff up. But know I will never share anything that is not in context with the word of God. If it is my opinion or my feeling based upon my interpretation, I will always share that.

Opening Scene:

Imagine, for a moment, that you have stepped into the opening frame of an extraordinary scene, a witness to a grand assembly unlike anything on earth. Before you, 24 resplendent beings stand arrayed in a circle around towering thrones that radiate with an otherworldly majesty. Each being is surrounded in an aura that shimmers with celestial light, their garments as white as the driven snow, untouched by any blemish of the mortal world.

The rumbling of their voices resounds through the expanse, each word they utter rolling with the booming power of distant thunder, vibrating the very air. The splendor before you defies language, transcending any spectacle you've known or could even attempt to articulate. It is an exquisite portrayal so vibrant, so alive with color and energy, that the lush palette of a film like "Avatar" pales, almost dull, in its shadow.

Amidst this visual symphony, your senses are gently caressed by an aroma that floats through the space, carrying with it an inexplicable joy. It seems to originate from your left, where the sacred incense from the offerings of the saints burns, its smoke spiraling upwards in a graceful dance. There is no guide to explain this to you, no sign to read, and yet, an innate knowledge fills your being; you understand intuitively the origin and significance of every detail around you.

Your heart burns in your chest, a wild rhythm that oscillates between trepidation and transcendent calm. Are you on the precipice of fear, or are you in a place of peace so profound that it banishes all trace of terror? In this moment, caught between the earthly and the divine, you might find yourself simultaneously bound to the edge of your seat and yet soaring—untethered, liberated from every worldly concern.

As you linger amidst the overwhelming glory of the scene, you notice a subtle but seismic shift in the atmosphere. The twenty-four elders, once statuesque in their poise, now adopt an air of deep reverence. Into this divine congress drifts a noticeable but unseen force, a mystery presence that commands attention without form. Your gaze searches for a source, for an identity, but there is only the profound impression of power that distinguishes this spirit from the rest, puzzling in its intentions.

Your mind races with questions, yet before you can tether your thoughts to any conclusion, the unthinkable happens. In a mere heartbeat, where once there was nothing, the likeness of a man emerges, emanating from the very essence of this powerful presence. As this figure takes its place at the core of the gathering, an instant recognition ignites within you: this is the sovereign, the architect of all that unfolds.

The scene before you seems to be orchestrated for your comprehension as if each detail were purposefully aligned with your arrival. Amidst the awe, an internal whisper surfaces, subtly betraying the depth of your wonder: "Is this place meant for me to witness?"

The extraordinariness of what unfolds before you challenges every idea of reality you've held. These beings who command such awe -- they bear no resemblance to any human or angelic form within the boundaries of your knowledge, prompting a silent, almost heretical question, "Are these gods?"

With each silent query, you stand witness to a pageant that stretches the very fabric of your understanding, leaving you to marvel at the unfathomable picture dancing before your entranced eyes.

The Roots found in Revelation

Narrative:

The vision that unfolds before you finds its roots in the Biblical passages of the New Testament, specifically in the Book of Revelation, Chapter 4, verses 1 to 6.

We read, "After this, I looked, and behold, a door standing open in heaven! And the first voice, which I had heard speaking to me like a trumpet, said, "Come up here, and I will show you what must take place after this." At once I was in the Spirit, and behold, a throne stood in heaven, with one seated on the throne.

And he who sat there had the appearance of jasper and carnelian, and around the throne was a rainbow that had the appearance of an emerald. Around the throne were twenty-four thrones, and seated on the thrones were twenty-four elders, clothed in white garments, with golden crowns on their heads.

From the throne came flashes of lightning, and rumblings and peals of thunder, and before the throne were burning seven torches of fire, which are the seven spirits of God, and before the throne, there was as it were a sea of glass, like crystal.

In the center, around the throne, were four living creatures, full of eyes in front and behind one like a lion, one like an ox, one with a face like a man, and one like an eagle in flight.

In this revelation, you are a sojourner, drawn into a vision of awe, a witness to the unfolding of a celestial drama scripted millennia ago, yet alive within the pages of sacred scripture.

The word "Elohim"

To fully grasp the identity and nature of these elders, we must acquaint ourselves with a term central to ancient theological discourse: "Elohim." This word, which resonates with the essence of divinity, signifies beings that are not of human origin. While "Elohim" can denote a single deity, it also possesses the flexibility to encompass multiple divine beings or gods when used in its plural form.

In the chapters to follow, we will look deeper into the multifaceted usage of "Elohim" throughout Biblical texts. However, for the purposes of our current discussion, it's important to appreciate how the term was perceived by the early Israelites, particularly during the Second Temple period.

Despite the word lending itself to a plural interpretation, this did not necessarily imply that the Israelites subscribed to polytheism, or the belief in multiple gods—at least not in a manner we would understand today.

What is evident, though, is their interpretation of the celestial picture, much like the one I have depicted, as an authentic reflection of the heavenly realm. This understanding did not conflict with their monotheistic principles but rather enriched their perception of the complex structure and order of the divine court as it was envisioned at the time.

Understanding How the Jewish Community Viewed Elohim

To comprehend the Israelites' conceptualization of "Elohim," it is instructive to trace their historical and cultural journey, particularly through the lens of their places of worship. In the writings of the Hebrew Bible, particularly 1 Kings Chapter 6, we encounter the origins of the First Temple.

Built during the zenith of Solomon's reign over the unified Israelite monarchy, this grand structure was completed around 957 BCE. It stood as a testament to the nation's religious devotion, surviving almost four centuries before meeting its demise at the hands of the Neo-Babylonian Empire, led by Nebuchadnezzar II, in 587/586 BCE.

The Books of Kings offer an elaborate account of the temple's construction, providing intimate details of its grandeur and the ritual practices of the Israelites. These narratives not only serve as a historical record but also shed light on the evolution of the Israelites' spiritual understanding and their relationship with the divine, which is deeply connected to the term "Elohim."

Through the prism of their temple worship, we gain insights into their evolving perception of the divine, a journey that further solidifies the place of "Elohim" within their theological framework.

Second Temple a Pivotal Change in History

The construction of the Second Temple marks a pivotal chapter in Israelite history. It rose from the ashes upon the return of the Israelites to their homeland, following their exile in Babylon. The cornerstone of this rebuilt sanctuary is believed to have been laid around 516 BCE, and it stood as the spiritual center of Jewish life until its destruction in 70 CE by the Romans.

During the approximately 600 years of the Second Temple's existence, significant theological and liturgical shifts occurred, deeply influencing the way the Israelites related to and worshiped God. These changes were not merely superficial adjustments; they represented a profound transformation in the collective spiritual consciousness of the people.

As we progress through the pages of this book, it is crucial to remember that Jesus lived and taught in the context of this Second Temple worldview. When He spoke to His disciples, He did so with an acute awareness of these shifts in understanding and perspective.

He engaged with the traditions and innovations of His time, fully cognizant of the new light in which his contemporaries viewed their faith and their relationship with the divine. This context is essential for interpreting His teachings and appreciating the cultural and religious landscape in which He operated.

6 Pivotal Changes that Reshaped Worship during the Second Temple.

Matthias Henze, a well-regarded scholar from Rice University with expertise in the study of Qumran and early Judaism, has identified six pivotal changes that reshaped worship during the Second Temple period.

He emphasizes, first and foremost, the cessation of the monarchy. In this era, the Israelites found themselves without a crown, navigating a reality starkly different from the kingly rule that characterized the First Temple period.

Concurrently, another significant shift was the end of prophecy. The voices of the prophets, once interwoven with the authority and narrative of the monarchy, fell silent. This cessation signaled a transformative moment in the religious landscape of Israel, altering the channels through which divine guidance and wisdom were sought and acknowledged.

Secondly, the Second Temple in Jerusalem, though central to worship, never quite attained the theological prominence or unifying authority held by its predecessor. In contrast to the First Temple, diverse groups began to distance themselves from the Second Temple's practices and authority.

The most famous among these were the sect responsible for the Dead Sea Scrolls. Opting for a life of asceticism, they withdrew to the Judean desert, choosing a self-imposed exile over alignment with the temple's rites, a testament to the evolving religious sentiments of the time.

Thirdly, the Second Temple era witnessed the normalization of Jewish life beyond the borders of Israel, firmly establishing their scattered culture as an enduring aspect of Jewish identity.

This historical shift is reflected in the Old Testament through narratives such as those found in the books of Esther and Daniel, which tell of Jewish experiences and challenges in foreign lands. These accounts underscore a significant broadening of the Jewish experience, as communities took root and flourished in diverse corners of the world.

Fourth, a hallmark of Second Temple Judaism was its increasing internal diversity and the pronounced splintering into various sects. This period was characterized by a proliferation of distinct groups within Judaism, each with its own interpretations and practices. The historian Josephus of the first century CE documents the emergence of three primary factions: the Pharisees, the Sadducees, and the Essenes.

However, current scholarship recognizes that the landscape was even more varied than these three well-known sects. Among these flourishing groups were the early followers of Jesus, who initially represented another sect within the broader Jewish tradition. It would only be after several centuries that Christianity would crystalize into a distinct religion separate from its Jewish roots.

Fifth, a transformative development occurred in the conveyance of divine wisdom: the transition from an oral tradition to the written word. This shift from momentary edification to the enduring written word not only preserved the messages attributed to God but also set the stage for the creation of the early biblical canons. The act of inscribing these once-spoken truths allowed for a tangible, accessible, and authoritative collection of scriptures to emerge, shaping the spiritual guidance of the community for generations to come.

Sixth, the Second Temple period was marked by an extraordinary surge in intellectual vigor, theological inquiry, and literary output. This time gave birth to a plethora of texts, with only a select few ultimately being incorporated into the canonical scriptures.

Among the numerous works authored during this time, two stand out for their enduring influence and will be the focus of the later discussions of this book: the Book of First Enoch and the Book of Jubilees. These writings, products of the rich tapestry of thought from this era, offer us a window into the spiritual and intellectual dynamism that characterized these centuries.

Fundamental understanding of Jesus in a Jewish context

Professor Henze goes on to say that for Christians to truly grasp the essence of Jesus and the intentions of those who penned the earliest accounts of His life, a fundamental understanding of Jesus' Jewish context is indispensable. Without an appreciation for early Judaism, one's comprehension of Jesus and His teachings may remain incomplete.

The challenge, however, lies in acknowledging that the religious practices and beliefs during Jesus' time diverged significantly from those documented in the Old Testament. The texts of the Old Testament, having been authored centuries before Jesus' ministry, are historical pillars that represent a distinct juncture in Israel's spiritual development.

To draw a modern parallel, it is compatible with attempting to define contemporary American society solely through the lens of the US Constitution; while foundational, it cannot fully sum up the nuanced evolution of a nation's present-day moral nature and practices.

To gain insight into the form of Judaism that Jesus practiced, our lens must focus on Jewish texts that were written closer to his time. It is within works such as the Book of First Enoch, the Book of Jubilees, and Fourth Ezra that we find the missing links spanning the chronological divide between the Old and the New Testament.

These texts provide invaluable context, painting a more complete picture of the religious landscape that shaped Jesus' life and teachings. They bridge the temporal expanse, offering a clearer understanding of the Judaism that was during the same time as Jesus.

Book of Enoch

Among the treasures of early Jewish literature, the Book of First Enoch stands out as a captivating apocalyptic work, richly recounting the tale of the fallen angels. This text is a testament to the vibrancy of early Jewish thought, replete with imaginative retellings of biblical narratives, vivid portrayals of celestial throne rooms, and the promise of a Messiah. It also takes readers on extraordinary journeys to the very edges of the known world.

While I refrain from deeming these texts as divinely inspired in a way that would warrant their formal inclusion in the biblical canon, their contextual alignment with the Bible cannot be overlooked. Hence, they serve as an enlightening compass, guiding us towards a more profound understanding of the perspective and beliefs held by those who lived in the biblical era.

Drawing from our insights into Second Temple thought, it is clear that Jewish conceptions of the divine maintained a monarchic structure, hinting at a belief in some sort of celestial hierarchy. The crux of the matter lies in their distinction between "Elohim" — a term encompassing divinity — and Yahweh, recognized as the singular, true, and living Creator God.

The discovery of the Dead Sea Scrolls in the Qumran caves has greatly enriched our understanding of how the term "Elohim" was comprehended within the Jewish community of that period. These ancient texts provide crucial context for interpreting the word beyond its surface meaning.

To engage with the Bible as it was understood by its original audience, it is therefore imperative to familiarize ourselves with this nuanced understanding. Grasping the distinction between "Elohim" and Yahweh, as perceived by the people of that time, allows us to read the scriptures through their eyes and interpret the sacred texts with a greater degree of historical and cultural accuracy.

To truly unravel the cosmic thread woven throughout the Bible, which unveils God's grand plan, it is essential to perceive the words within the Scriptures as the Israelites themselves would have understood them. Appreciating the biblical texts in this contextual light is the key to a deeper understanding of the intricate tapestry that chronicles the divine narrative.

Psalms 82:1 on Elohim

As we conclude this chapter, let's cast a brief glance at Psalms 82:1, which employs the term "Elohim" in a fascinating context. This verse opens the door to an intriguing concept, one that I believe sheds light on the identity of the 24 elders mentioned in the Book of Revelation—the divine council.

The verse reads: *"God has taken his place in the divine council; in the midst of the gods, he holds judgment."*

Here, we encounter a celestial hierarchy, and within this singular verse, "Elohim" is used distinctly, referencing two different entities. It juxtaposes "God (Elohim)," who assumes a position within the divine council, with "the gods (Elohim)," over whom He presides in judgment.

It's clear that the verse delineates between a superior Elohim and others who are lesser. From this, we can infer that the premier Elohim refers to the supreme Creator, Yahweh, while the other usage of "Elohim" likely pertains to the 24 elders depicted in Revelation 4.

This distinction is pivotal to our understanding of the structured divine assembly portrayed in these ancient texts.

To review what we read earlier in this chapter, the idea of a group of divine beings collaborating with Yahweh was not only known by the Jews but also by Jesus.

The 24 elders, whom you glimpsed at this chapter's outset, collaborate with God in dispensing judgment over humanity. Like many, I had once breezed past these verses without fully appreciating the notion that God engages a council in His governance. It's my aspiration that this revelation becomes clear to you as well, illuminating your reading of the scriptures in the following chapters.

In the previous chapter, we discussed the three grand rebellions and mentioned Watchers as divine beings. The divine council is distinct from these beings. The divine council is a part of the ruling party that oversaw these grand rebellions with Yahweh. We mentioned them here in the early chapters to give context to what you will read in future chapters.

To deepen our understanding of this celestial assembly, let's proceed to our next chapter, 'Witness to the Divine Council,' where we'll further dissect the roles these entities play in the unfolding of God's grand narrative.

Chapter 4

Witness to the Divine Council

Opening Scene:

Your eyes wide with wonder, as you step tentatively onto hallowed ground, transported beyond the veil of the temporal world into the heart of divinity itself. The air shimmers with a sacred stillness as you drink in the unfathomable beauty that unfurls around you.

Above, creation's tapestry stretches into infinity, a celestial sphere that hums with the praise of constellations. Their harmonious song is a poem to the wonders of the Lord, an eternal melody of his steadfast faithfulness. It resonates with the timbre of the divine, a sound so pure it resonates within your very soul.

Before you lie the assembly of the holy ones, a congregation of powerful beings poised with solemn grace. Their garments, woven from the fabric of dawn's first light, flutter gently, defying the confines of earthly physics. Each countenance is serene, yet their eyes hold the wisdom of ages, windows illuminating the expanse of knowledge they possess.

"The great assembly," you breathe, the words a mere whisper, an attempt to name the celestial court that convenes before the majesty of the Almighty. The atmosphere is charged with reverence, "heaven's court" in session, a gathering of those chosen to stand in counsel with the Most High.

Your gaze falls upon the heart of the assembly, where the splendor of the throne overtakes every sense. The visage of the Lord, though shrouded in ineffable glory, commands the space with a presence that whispers both love and authority. Around him, the figures of the holy ones stand in stark silhouette against the divine radiance that crowns him.

"Hear the judgment," one voice announces, resonant and clear, breaking the solemn hush. The "divine council" draws closer, their focus sharp as they anticipate the unfolding of decrees forged in the celestial gavel's fall.

Time seems to stand still as you witness, breath held in sacred pause, the majesty of divine order at work. It is a dance of destiny and devout deliberation, a process inscrutable yet undeniably just.

And there, in the midst of "His own congregation," truth unfurls with the slow grace of dawn's arrival, and you, a mere mortal awash in the echo of the divine, being irrevocably changed. Standing on the brink of heaven and earth, you are privy to the marvel and mystery of the cosmos — a world invisible to many, yet revealed to you in this extraordinary moment.

The divine council, arrayed in celestial splendor, deliberates with the weight of eternity in their words, casting judgments that ripple through the universe. The impact resonates within you, as each pronouncement shapes the fabric of reality, weaving justice and mercy into the very essence of being.

Enraptured by the gravity of the scene, you sense a profound connection to something greater than yourself, a thread binding your spirit to the divine narrative unfolding before you. The holy ones, in their solemnity and grandeur, are the stewards of a cosmic order that transcends human comprehension, yet here, in their presence, you are an observer to this sacred dance of governance and wisdom.

In this confluence of spiritual majesty, you find yourself humbled, a quiet spectator at the threshold of the infinite. The divine council's work is a testament to the omnipotence of the Lord, a reflection of His perfection mirrored in the faces of the assembly.

As they move with purpose, informed by an unseen choreography, you are reminded of the Old Testament passage of Psalms 89:5 which says *"Let the heavens praise your wonders, O Lord, your faithfulness in the assembly of the holy ones!"* This hinting at such splendor, is now vividly alive before you.

This experience is indeed overwhelming, a cascade of feelings washes over you, leaving you struggling to reconcile the emotions stirring within. Just as you begin to grasp this profound encounter, you find yourself swiftly transported to another time frame, further unfolding the layers of this transcendent journey.

Stepping into the Shoes of the Prophet Isaiah

Narrative:

Imagine, if you will, stepping into the same realm as the prophet Isaiah, entering a chamber where the divine and the earthly intersect, as recounted in Isaiah 6:1-7. Picture finding yourself in the midst of the heavenly court, face to face with the sublime. Together, let us ponder the passage and place ourselves within its narrative, wondering how we might react if we were to stand in Isaiah's shoes.

"In the year of King Uzziah's passing, I beheld a vision of the Lord on His throne, exalted and magnificent; His regal train enveloped the sanctuary. Hovering above Him were the seraphim, majestic creatures each possessing six wings: two veiling their faces in reverence, two cloaking their feet in humility, and with two, they soared aloft. They called to one another, their voices resounding the refrain:

'Holy, holy, holy is the Lord Almighty;

the entire earth is awash with His glory.'

At that proclamation, the very foundations trembled, and clouds of incense flooded the space. Overwhelmed, I cried out: 'Woe to me! I am undone. I am a man of impure speech, among a people with the same; yet my eyes have gazed upon the King, the Lord Almighty.'

In response, a seraph approached me swiftly, holding a glowing ember, plucked with tongs from the altar. The coal grazed my lips, and the seraph declared: 'See, this has touched your lips; your iniquity is removed, and your sin is accounted for.'

This scripture draws us into the awe and terror Isaiah must have felt in the unprecedented honor of such an encounter. Much like the vivid scenario we conjured in our opening scene—a tapestry woven from the threads of our imagination—Isaiah, too, found himself immersed in a very real and tangible experience. While our minds painted an imaginary landscape of the divine council, for Isaiah, the encounter of the throne room was an undeniable reality.

Just as we were left awestruck and without words by the power of our envisioned scene, Isaiah stood similarly speechless in the wake of his profound and authentic vision. As we now unpack Isaiah's words, let our own senses and emotions intertwine with the vision, allowing us to grasp but a sliver of the depth that is meeting the divine.

Exploration of Awe and Authority

It seems reasonable to conclude that, were we to find ourselves amid the divine council, we might feel as Isaiah did— an overwhelming sense of being out of place amidst such holiness. This presence of the divine council is affirmed by the passage in Revelation 4:10, which it states, *"The twenty-four elders fall down before him who is seated on the throne and worship him who lives forever and ever."*

This attests to the reverence and awe that pervades the atmosphere in the presence of the divine, an experience that would undoubtedly lead us to echo Isaiah's sentiments of humility and profound veneration.

Isaiah's vision of the heavenly throne room resonates within this context. Despite his best efforts to encapsulate the awe-inspiring encounter with words, it is likely that language itself fell short of capturing the full magnitude of what he experienced.

Confronted with the divine council, Isaiah could only express a profound sense of his own unworthiness, recognizing his lack of holiness when measured against such grandeur. This divine assembly epitomizes a level of power and majesty that eclipses our earthly understanding—ruling with unquestionable authority and embodying eternal perfection beyond our wildest imaginings.

Where, then, do we stand in our quest to comprehend the divine council? How should we approach this concept to gain a clearer understanding? Let us look deeper into these questions, unpacking the term 'divine council' as scholars of Hebrew and Semitic studies interpret it.

Scholars Interpretation of Divine Council

Scholars describe the divine council as a celestial assembly—a pantheon of divine entities gathered in council to govern the workings of the cosmos.

Bear in mind that the idea of a divine council was not unique to Israel but was a common motif among ancient Mediterranean cultures. Yet, the divine council as depicted within the Israelite religion, particularly through the Psalms, bore distinctive features. Scholar Michael Heiser points out that comprehending the particular structure of the Israelite divine council yields considerable insight into our understanding of God and the spiritual realm as articulated in biblical theology.

In terms of their function, we can surmise that the divine council convened to oversee the execution of God's directives, ensuring that humanity aligns with Yahweh's flawless design.

There exists another scriptural passage in the Book of Job, specifically 38:4-7, that provides valuable context for the concept of the divine council. This excerpt discusses the celestial realm prior to the creation of the earth, and it introduces two distinct terms: "morning stars" and "sons of God." In this context, God addresses Job with a series of rhetorical questions that underscore human limitation in the face of divine majesty:

"Where were you when I laid the earth's foundation? Speak if you have understanding. Who set its measurements, since you surely know? Or who stretched the measuring line across it? On what were its footings set, or who laid its cornerstone—while the morning stars sang together, and all the sons of God shouted for joy?"

Through these verses, we are invited to contemplate the grandeur of creation and the exultant chorus of the divine beings that were present at the dawn of the material universe.

As we ponder the passage from Job, it becomes evident that God exists beyond the confines of human time, with the creation of humanity coming after His own eternal presence—a truth He emphasizes to Job.

However, let us steer our focus towards a particular verse that may not be as readily understood as others: Verse 7. This passage invites deeper inquiry: Who are the "morning stars" and the "sons of God," and why do they express their joy so fervently? What part do they play in relation to the divine council? Could they be the same as the twenty-four elders mentioned in Revelation 4, or does this imply a broader pantheon beyond them?

While one might yearn for definitive answers to these questions, the truth is that the Bible does not elaborate on this aspect. We are left to speculate and interpret, recognizing the limits of our understanding when faced with the mysteries preserved within the sacred scriptures.

What can be discerned from Job 38:7 is a distinction between the *"morning stars"* and the *"sons of God."* The term *"morning star"* has been used to refer to Jesus, as seen in Revelation 22:16, 2 Peter 1:19, and Revelation 2:28. Regarding the *"sons of God"*, or 'beney Elohim' in Hebrew, we can ascertain that these beings are not human.

This verse suggests that God, accompanied by His mighty celestial beings, existed prior to the creation of the world. It appears they rejoiced with exultant shouts as creation reached its majestic culmination. They were, in essence, celestial witnesses to Yahweh's act of bringing the world into existence as we know it.

Most biblical scholars would not equate the 'sons of God' with angels, as the Hebrew term 'mal'ak' specifically denotes a messenger. In the ancient Semitic worldview, the phrase 'sons of God' was employed to designate divine beings endowed with significant responsibilities or realms of authority, suggesting a rank above the mere delivery of messages.

The term 'angel' conveys the critical, yet more limited, role of serving as a divine messenger. The portrayal of the 'sons of God' in the scripture hints at their existence as a higher order of divine beings. This raises the intriguing question: might they represent a distinct class within the celestial hierarchy, possessing divine attributes of their own as a god?

Ancient civilizations revered the stars as the resplendent manifestation of divine beings inhabiting realms beyond human reach. While there are manifold uncertainties surrounding their exact nature, it is reasonable to believe these entities are creations of Yahweh, vested with an extraordinary measure of power and authority. It's understandable, then, that such divine beings might be mistaken for gods, given their clear distinction from humanity in both might and nature.

The term *"sons of God"* recurs throughout the Bible, not solely in the Book of Job. As we advance through subsequent chapters, we will further explore instances of this term to provide deeper context. Yet, the essential insight we should glean from Job 38 is the acknowledgment of a heavenly court, a divine council that shared in the wonders of creation alongside God, long before the earth was formed.

Unveiling the Reality of Lesser gods

In the past, when I encountered references to other gods in the scriptures, I assumed they were mere figments of human imagination, crafted by hand and then revered by those who made them. The Bible frequently warns against the worship of graven images, instructing us not to prostrate ourselves before them.

Consequently, whenever I encountered such verses, I dismissed the idea that these gods held any genuine existence or power. However, as we look deeper and provide further context for these so-called gods in the chapters ahead, you and I may start to recognize that they could indeed possess authentic might.

What came to my mind as I wrote this, is that many of us carry a cross around our neck, some have a picture hanging of Jesus in their house. Are those not carved images? are those not made by man so we can be reminded of our God? We believe our God is real and so did all these other nations that are mentioned in the bible. Like I have mentioned in previous chapters there is a lot more to this story than what we originally understood.

As we conclude this chapter, let us revisit a verse from Psalm 82 that we examined in the previous chapter. Recall the scripture: "God has taken His place in the divine council; in the midst of the gods he holds judgment:"

To delve deeper into this passage, it's crucial to note the dual use of the word "God," both times translated from "Elohim." We understand that the initial instance of "Elohim" refers to Yahweh, the Creator of all. The subsequent "Elohim" however, denotes other divine beings. One point I did not provide context for in the last chapter is the significance of the suffix "-im" in Hebrew, which is a linguistic indicator of plurality. Therefore, when we come across "Elohim," we are in fact referring to more than one divine entity.

Returning to an earlier contemplation, we might question if there exists more than one god. Our readings have indicated the presence of a council comprising beings of substantial might, superior in rank to angels. Could we, then, appropriately refer to these entities as gods with a lowercase 'g'?

This distinction is made to suggest that while they are divine, their capabilities, especially in terms of creation, may not match the omnipotence of Yahweh. Nevertheless, this is speculative, considering the Bible does not detail all their potential powers.

It seems reasonable, for the sake of clarity in our upcoming discussions, to use the term 'lowercase g gods' when referring to these distinguished beings. This terminology aids in distinguishing them from Yahweh while acknowledging their significant roles within the divine hierarchy.

Moreover, it seems justifiable to assert that these beings are not mere angelic messengers, as typically depicted in the Bible. With this understanding, let's draw this chapter to a close. We've come to learn that Yahweh, the Creator God, presides over an assembly of lowercase 'g' gods.

The scriptural reference to 'sons of God' indeed alludes to divine beings of considerable stature. In this context, it becomes clear that these lowercase 'g' gods, created by Yahweh—though the full extent of their nature remains hidden—are entrusted with significant oversight over humanity and the universe, serving within what might be considered His divine council.

The question of whether there are more than twenty-four lowercase 'g' gods remains open; the possibility certainly exists. As we move forward in the following chapters, we will continue to put together God's Grand Plan and understand how His Divine council plays a role in revealing the thread of love that runs through the narrative.

Consider these initial chapters as pieces of a mosaic, and within this particular chapter on God's divine council, we find an essential piece that helps us grasp His profound love for us. As stated in 1 John 4:16, *"God is love"*, suggesting that His divine council, too, must rule with love at its core.

To grasp the full impact of Jesus' resurrection, it is essential to acknowledge the existence of a celestial domain that governs and makes decisions—a reality that transcends our conventional perception of time. While numerous authors delve deeply into the intricacies of this divine council, the purpose of our brief exploration here has been to sketch the broader canvas, illustrating the depth of Jesus' love for humanity within this greater cosmic framework.

In the next chapter, our journey takes us to the tranquil beauty of the Garden of Eden, where we will explore the embodiment of divine love as it's revealed in the story of Creation. We will also encounter the divine council once more, uncovering the initial grand rebellion—a cosmic upheaval that Jesus' resurrection ultimately overturned.

Now that we have established a foundation, we are well-positioned to go into the greater unfolding of God's majestic blueprint through the ensuing narratives.

Chapter 5

The Garden of Eden Unraveling the Divine Image

Opening Scene:

Fade in on a vision that transcends mere imagination, as you, the silent observer, step into the opening chapter of this new world—a garden that defies every known precept of beauty. The hues that bloom around you are not of our earthly palette; they radiate with resplendence, their glow casting a graceful light on the sprawling Eden that captures you.

The air is filled with the symphony of conversation, its source, a shimmering waterfall that seems to flow not just with water, but with life itself. As you draw closer, the figures of a man and woman come into view. Yet, their presence suggests they are not alone—a chorus of unseen voices accompanies their dialogue.

In this garden, the man and the woman are unclothed, but it is unlike any notion of nakedness you know of—there is no sense of shame, no undercurrent of illicit desire. Theirs is the epitome of purity, an embodiment of innocence that feels as natural and undisturbed as the world itself. Here, in this moment, you witness the original state of humanity —unmarred, unashamed, and in perfect harmony with the vast creation around them.

As you edge further into the scene, a sense of déjà vu washes over you—the presence that first revealed itself in the previous chapters now resurfaces, not as a corporeal entity, but as an intangible essence of spirit. It's a challenging sensation to articulate, yet the certainty that you're amidst not one but a multitude of these spiritual presences is undeniable. Your initial confusion, sparked by this unparalleled experience, soon yields to profound emotion.

Surrounded by this all-consuming love, tears of joy cascade down your cheeks. Every fiber of your existence resonates with a deep-seated longing—you yearn to belong to this place, to be a part of its untainted grace. The question burns within you, an inextinguishable flame: How might you secure your passage to this celestial garden? What steps must you take to be granted entry into this sublime haven?

Longing For Divine Fellowship

Narrative:

In Genesis chapter 3, we are introduced to God's primeval design—a vision where man and all of creation exist in harmonious fellowship with the Divine, meant to stretch into eternity. It seems to be a universal cry echoing within humanity, this innate desire to return to the splendor of the garden. Although I do not claim to be a psychologist, my studies indicate a commonality among all humans: an insatiable desire within us to feel loved.

People across the globe yearn for acceptance, yearn for peace, and seek purpose that imbues their lives with meaning. The Garden of Eden once satisfied these yearnings flawlessly, without a hint of absence or want.

Yet, with humanity's decision to step away from this ideal state due to sin, a cataclysmic shift occurred. The sacred purity of fellowship was breached; God found it necessary to withdraw from direct communion with His creation.

However, as we traverse the upcoming chapters of this book, a thread of hope emerges. We will discover that from the earliest moments of fallibility, God had already set in motion a plan to reconcile, mend the rupture, and rekindle the fellowship with humankind that once flourished in the garden.

Contemplations on Choice and Temptation

Genesis chapter 3 serves as a crucial canvas, painting the stark dichotomy of good versus evil, and life against death—dualities that crescendo in humanity's descent from grace. If it has been a while since you last read the narrative of

Genesis 3 for yourself, I recommend revisiting it now before you continue reading. Doing so will provide clarity and perspective for the reflections contained within this chapter.

As you read into Chapter 3, it is apparent that Adam and Eve's fateful choice to defy God was not made in isolation. It prompts me to ponder: Had the serpent, a being of divine origin with evil intent, not weaved his seductive web within Eden, would our forebearers still have reached for the forbidden fruit?

This question resists an unequivocal answer, yet it stirs the mind with wonder. If you find yourself, much like me, intrigued by the complexities of free will and temptation, then let us muse together on this primordial crossroad.

What I firmly believe is that this evil supernatural creature had predetermined that his desires and designs would supersede those of Yahweh's. The subsequent alliance of mankind with this cunning spirit in rebellion against God irrevocably altered the original essence and function of the Garden of Eden.

The tangible acquisition of knowledge of good and evil by Adam and Eve suggests that the tempter's promises, while catastrophically misguided, contained elements of truth.

This is further underscored when God Himself confirms the transformation of man's understanding in Genesis 3:22, acknowledging, *"Behold, the man has become like one of us in knowing good and evil."* This pivotal verse warrants further exploration, which we shall undertake later in this chapter.

The Freedom of Choice

At this juncture, it is clear that God's pristine intention for creation was redirected as a direct outcome of His love, manifest through the gift of free will bestowed upon humankind. This freedom empowered mankind to navigate between the options that were divinely presented.

The question arises: if God is omniscient and aware of all possibilities before they unfold, wouldn't He have foreseen the choice that humanity would make? Indeed, as God, He possesses comprehensive knowledge of all that is yet to occur, yet this foreknowledge does not negate the agency He grants us.

The act of knowing in advance does not equate to predestination. The divine foresight of a choice does not determine that choice—free will remains absolute, held in tension with the sovereignty of an all-knowing God.

God's love is wholeheartedly complete, and within that completeness is His desire for authentic reciprocity—a yearning for His creation to love Him freely, not out of compulsion. We were not fashioned as robots, preprogrammed to execute His bidding devoid of choice. He embodies gentleness, kindness, and boundless patience, seeking a relationship with us that arises from genuine desire, not from mandated obligation.

Ephesians 3:18-19 speaks to the immeasurable dimensions of God's love—it is wide, long, high, and deep, surpassing our ability to fully grasp its magnitude. The essence of this love is not just to overwhelm us with its vastness, but as verse 19 clarifies, to complete us with all the fullness of life and potency that stems solely from Him.

Do you have a strong desire to be recognized and loved for who you truly are? I do, and now I fully understand that God is the only one capable of fulfilling that need in its purest form. My choices either allow me to experience this love or leave me wanting, searching in places where it can never be found.

The Divine Dwelling Before the Fall

To deepen our understanding of Eden, we must immerse ourselves in its state before the fall. Picture the Garden of Eden as the breathtaking landscape I previously depicted—a locale pulsing with otherworldly splendor.

Biblical scholar Jonathan L. suggests that for those in the biblical era, the Garden was perceived not merely as horticulture but as a realm transcending the ordinary. In their eyes, Eden would have resembled a temple, regarded as the dwelling place of deities. To them, Eden represented God's terrestrial footstool, an extension of the celestial domain.

Adding to this perspective, scholar Wenham suggests that since Adam shared communion with God within Eden, the Garden served as a temporal counterpart to the eternal pattern. Passages like Genesis 2:6, 8-9, and 10-16 depict Eden as a lushly irrigated abode, with Ezekiel 28:14 portraying it as a holy mountain. To the ancients reading these texts, the Garden emerged as the quintessential sanctuary, a consecrated realm where the divine and human worlds converged in beautiful harmony.

Reflecting on the insights from our last chapter, one might speculate whether the Garden of Eden also served as the assembly ground for the divine council. The serpent's temptation of Eve, as recounted in Genesis 3:5, hints at this possibility. The serpent entices her by saying, *"God knows that when you eat of it your eyes will be opened, and you will be like God [elōhîm], knowing good and evil."*

Building on the groundwork laid by biblical scholar Michael Heiser, let's examine this more closely. Heiser indicates that the term ʾelōhîm in this context isn't singular but rather plural, as becomes evident when analyzing Genesis 3:22.

In this verse, God does not address Adam, Eve, or the serpent, but rather remarks, *"Behold, the man has become like one of us in knowing good and evil. Now, lest he reach out his hand and take also of the tree of life and eat, and live forever."* The notion of Adam and Eve ascending to a station *"like one of us"* unmistakably implies a collective—a plurality.

Therefore, the ʾelōhîm referenced in verse 5 suggests a congregation and not a solitary entity. This persuasive inference leads us back to the question at hand: Might the Garden of Eden have been more than a paradise for the first humans, possibly acting as the meeting place for God's divine council?

Some who venture through these passages might initially understand the phrase "one of us" as an allusion to the

Trinity rather than a divine council. This interpretation has resonated with me throughout my adult life until a closer examination of the original language prompted me to reflect anew.

Let's look into this nuance, starting with Genesis 1:1-25, where the text affirms that God single-handedly creates the heavens and the earth, pronouncing His work as good. Yet, in verse 26, there emerges a remarkable shift in language: "Let us make man in our image, after our likeness." The use of "our" captures our attention and beckons us to ask—who does "our" represent?

As discussed, "our" seems to invite the concept of a divine council rather than a solitary divine being. While the idea of the Trinity, as a unity of Father, Son, and Holy Spirit, has traditionally provided an explanation for this plurality, the oneness of the Trinity does pose a question: Why would God refer to "our" if the Trinity inherently signifies a single entity?

Reflecting on Jesus' words in John 14:9, *"Whoever has seen me has seen the Father,"* and His affirmation in John 10:30, *"I and the Father are one,"* we affirm the oneness of the Trinity. Hence, if the Trinity represents a singular divinity, the gesture to "our" in Genesis seems more plausible as a reference to the council of divine beings within God's heavenly domain.

This interpretation reconciles the scriptural portrayal of a singular God with a scene of reverent consultation. How else can we interpret such a rich tapestry of divine interaction, if not in this way?

In the Divine Likeness

With a clearer understanding of the "our" from the previous discussion, we now direct our focus to Genesis 1:26 and the mysterious directive, *"Let us make man in our image."* The question at hand is this: What does it mean to be made in the *"image of God"*? This pivotal phrase surfaces multiple times within Genesis (Gen 1:26-27; 5:1-3; 9:6) and warrants a closer inspection. Notably, it is a designation bestowed equally upon men and women, without extending to any other earthly creatures.

Scholar Michael Heiser provides insight, suggesting that the *"image of God"* is an inherent quality that all humans possess equally, setting them apart distinctly from the rest of creation.

Historically, theologians have ventured numerous interpretations of what being made in God's image might entail. Many have said that it relates to characteristics akin to the divine, such as intellect, rationality, emotion, free will, consciousness, self-awareness, and the capability for communication and prayer—all faculties seemingly linked to the operations of the human brain.

Yet this raises a complex issue: not all human beings manifest these attributes in equal measure or at all times. For example, a developing fetus within the womb or an individual in a state of brain death would not actively exhibit these cognitive functions. Thus, we must consider these nuances as we attempt to fathom the full depths of what it means to be created in the image of an infinite God.

God, His divine council, and humanity share a commonality through their distinctive attributes—a truth that becomes ever clearer after the fall. These traits, which include intelligence, rational thinking, emotions, willpower, awareness, and the capacity for prayer, enable human beings to engage in communion with the Divine.

The "Image of God" is a distinguishing endowment that sets humans apart from all other forms of life, a gift exclusively bestowed upon mankind. This divine image is implanted wholly, not incrementally, for Genesis 9:6 suggests that it is precisely the "Image of God" that imparts sacred value to human life. Were this image to be merely fragmentary, it would imply that life, too, holds only fragmented sanctity.

On a personal note, I would have preferred blissful ignorance, living in uninterrupted fellowship with God for eternity. However, with the knowledge that I have now, there's a certain allure in recognizing that we embody the complete, not partial, image of God—that our very existence is consecrated.

The Divine Plan for Fellowship

Revisiting the origins of the Garden of Eden, Genesis 2:8 establishes the scene: *"The Lord God planted a garden in Eden, in the east, and there He put the man whom He had formed."* While it's paramount to remember that God's act of creation spanned the entire Earth, He bestowed particular attention upon a sanctified place known as Eden, situated in the east. This deliberate choice underlines the profound significance of the garden—a sentiment echoed by many biblical scholars.

Eden was more than just a part of creation; it was a divine sanctuary set apart from the world, designed for communion between God's heavenly council and humanity. In the quietude of Eden's garden, documented in Genesis 3:8, mankind stood witness to the presence of the Lord God, walking in the cool of the day. It was here, amidst the verdant splendor of Eden, that all of creation—both the divine and the human—converged in harmonious fellowship.

From the inception of time, it was God's heartfelt intent to dwell alongside His creation; He aspired to be our God in a world where separation was foreign. This fundamental aspiration is captured in Genesis 3:22, which underscores our intended destiny: to share in eternal life with our Creator. God never envisioned a reality where we would be distanced from His constant presence.

The portrayal of Jesus as the consummate image of God in the New Testament is indeed no mere happenstance. As disciples walking in God's path, we are called to emulate Christ's example. This relationship between Jesus and His followers is illuminated through passages such as 2 Corinthians 4:4 and Colossians 1:15, where Christ is depicted as the living embodiment of the God we encounter in the Hebrew Scriptures.

Thus, if we accept that Jesus is the manifestation of Yahweh in human form, the New Testament clarifies that He serves as the divine image and archetype of humanity. Philippians 2:7 reinforces this notion, explaining that Jesus, though divine, assumed a mortal likeness, "found in appearance as a man." This act of incarnation positions Jesus as the quintessential imager—a perfect reflection of the Divine for humanity to both witness and aspire toward, as expanded upon in the greater context of Philippians 2:1–11.

The Path to Divine Likeness

Romans 8:29 invites us into a transformative process, where we are beckoned to mold ourselves into the image of the Son. This call to likeness, however, should not be mistaken for a future physical resemblance to Jesus in a celestial realm. Instead, it signifies an aspirational molding of our inner selves, a shaping of our thoughts, actions, and how we navigate life's myriad situations to mirror Jesus' own.

This inner metamorphosis is a gradual and lifelong endeavor. Paul, in his epistle, encapsulates this spiritual evolution: *"And we all, with unveiled face, beholding the glory of the Lord, are being transformed into the same image from one degree of glory to another. For this comes from the Lord who is the Spirit"* (2 Corinthians 3:18). This passage assures us that as we gaze upon God's glory, without barriers, we are steadily transfigured to resemble that divine image more closely—a work that the Spirit orchestrates within us.

Complementing this, in 1 Corinthians 15:49, Paul reminds us of our dual heritage as beings of both earth and heaven: *"Just as we have borne the image of the man of dust, we shall also bear the image of the man of heaven."* It is a profound reminder that our transformation into divine likeness is not only our destiny but our origin, as we transition from reflecting our earthly genesis to embracing our heavenly calling.

Rediscovering Divine Fellowship

As we turn the last page of this chapter, it's a moment to reflect on the profound truths we've encountered. Our journey of understanding has brought us to a pivotal recognition: the fall of humanity in the Garden of Eden was not just a transgression, but a disruption of the sacred fellowship that God had lovingly established with us.

We've come to see that the divine realm and humanity once shared a direct communion, with the divine council holding its sacred assemblies alongside God in the serenity of Eden.

From the breach caused by the fall, we've come to acknowledge our unique identity as image bearers of the Divine, molded in the very likeness of our Creator. Yet, amidst the revelations of past missteps, we've unearthed a glimmer of hope—the unwavering purpose of God to renew our fellowship to its initial glory.

As we tread further along the path laid out by scriptures, the subsequent chapters promise to unfurl more of this restorative blueprint, piecing together the vast tapestry that is God's grand narrative.

The next installment will scrutinize the consequences of Adam and Eve's sin, their fall, and the profound implications on human history—the intricate patterns that will enrich our spiritual mosaic as this book unfolds.

Chapter 6

Consequences to Mankind's Sin

Opening Scene:

As the new chapter begins, envision yourself being transported to an unknown land—a landscape that continues to radiate beauty with its variety of colors and lush green vegetation. The distant murmur of a river reaches your ears, the sound is both soothing and invigorating. Yet, as you allow your gaze to wander, a subtle realization dawns on you: this place lacks the vibrancy and the luminous quality of the garden you remember.

A sense of wistfulness washes over you as the stark contrast becomes apparent. Here, the colors, though present, seem muted; the land, though rich, is tinged with signs of uncertainty. Where once stood the idealized perfection of a garden, tended by divine hands, now lies a wilderness that calls out for care and cultivation.

Your journey is marked by a physical toll unseen in the prior landscape of bliss. The soles of your feet bear the testament of a challenging terrain, marked with blisters from the lengthy wandering. Your body, a vessel of resilience, signals to you through aches unfamiliar, a stark reminder of the new reality you face.

No longer does the omnipotent Gardner oversee the growth and harmony of His creation. Instead, the responsibility has shifted upon your shoulders, an inheritance of the fall. Tasks that were once unknowingly fulfilled by divine providence now rest squarely in the realm of your human effort. There lies before you an unyielding land, ready to be shaped by your toil and perseverance—a profound departure from the garden you once knew.

Now, in this rugged expanse, the onus to sustain yourself rests heavily upon your shoulders. Gone are the days when sustenance sprang forth effortlessly from the earth. Today, you must engage in the primal act of the hunt, foraging, and capturing your meals amidst the wilderness.

Communication with the Spirit, once a constant and comforting presence, has become tenuous, as if a gulf has stretched between you. The immediacy of spiritual intimacy you once took for granted seems to have recessed into a distant memory. In your heart, you labor to bridge the disconnection, yearning to reclaim the closeness that once bathed your days in peace.

Repeatedly, you find your steps drawn to the borders of the garden, that lost paradise, yet each attempt to penetrate its barriers ends in futility. Inside, a battle wages—a struggle between rationalizing your fateful decision and confronting the piercing truth that you long to undo it. Amidst this turmoil, unbidden tears breach the banks of your eyes, giving voice to the profound sorrow gnawing at your soul.

Overwhelmed by a tide of hopelessness, guilt, and shame, you collapse to your knees, the burden of sin bowing you to the earth itself. In this abyss of despair, an epiphany arises, crystallizing in your mind with resounding clarity: you were never meant to taste this bitter fruit of anguish; it's an inheritance of the fall, not of your creation.

With this realization, the Spirit, though distant, sends a shimmer of illumination to your weary heart. Eyes opened a new, you perceive a truth that was always there—that this pained existence, this estrangement from the Divine, was never God's intention for His beloved.

It's a recognition that pierces through the cloud of your sorrow, revealing a fragment of shared grief: the Spirit, too, mourns the chasm that sin has carved between you, for the heart of your Creator was broken by the very same choice that now haunts your existence.

The Divine Design for Fellowship

Narrative:

At the heart of creation lies a fundamental element of God's blueprint: the desire for intimate, sacred communion with His works. God is the embodiment of pure, unbounded love—a love that extends impartially to all His divine beings and to humanity. Above all, God seeks not a transactional, rule-bound association with us, but a profound and affectionate bond.

This desire for deep, heartfelt connection reflects the very nature of God, a longing for us to reciprocate with equivalent fervor the love He generously bestows upon us. However, when sin made its insidious entry into this harmonic equation, it cleaved the close-knit relationship God cherished with His creation.

Divinity, defined by its inherent holiness, cannot coexist with sin, and thus this love, so freely given, faced an unforeseen rift that challenged the very possibility of communion.

The Role of the Deceiver

It was the deception of Satan that laid the foundation for the rupture of this divine kinship. As recounted in Isaiah 14, the entity known as Lucifer sought to exalt himself to the station of the Most High, initiating an insurrection against a benevolent God.

Later identified by the apostle Paul in 2 Corinthians 4:4 as the "god of this age," Satan exploited his understanding of the divine to lure humanity into a trap, presenting Eve with a truth stripped of its dire repercussions.

Amid the cunning temptation presented in Eden, we are compelled to ponder an alternate history. Had the serpent refrained from beguiling Eve, would the sanctity of our communion with God have remained unscathed?

Would the narrative of salvation, culminating in the life and sacrificial mission of Jesus Christ, ever have been necessitated? These questions probe the depths of theological inquiry, contemplating a world that might have been but was not.

While the hypothetical scenario of an Eden untouched by temptation remains locked in the realm of the unknown, our understanding of the events that transpired rests on firmer ground. The serpent's strategy entailed merely hinting at untold aspects of God's forbidding. By suggesting that partaking of the forbidden fruit would render Eve more godlike, he ignited a spark of curiosity within her.

It was a curiosity inflamed by the suggestion of hidden knowledge, of wisdom that lay beyond the boundary of the divine command. Satan played upon this curiosity, insinuating that should Eve seek to access the esoteric insights, she would have to defy God's specific directive. The allure of the undisclosed was potent, tempting Eve with the notion that true enlightenment required her to transgress.

As Eve pondered the fruit, her mind began to weave a veil of rationalization, convincing herself that the act she contemplated might not be so grievous. The thought took hold that perhaps God would ultimately understand her decision, that it was a small step, not the monumental defiance it was. This subtle inner negotiation set the stage for the fateful consequences that would unravel from her hand's next motion.

Satan, with his arsenal of cunning and deceit, recognized the moment Eve's justifications began to ease her doubts;

he knew he had ensnared her. Edging ever closer to the fruit, she heard Satan's reassurances that becoming "like" God, infused with the knowledge of good and evil, aligned with God's own desires—and that, contrary to divine warning, she would not face death for her actions.

It was the crucial tipping point; his words, dripping with guile, were enough. Compelled by the twisted promise of enlightenment and divinity, Eve succumbed and tasted the forbidden fruit. In that instant, Satan reveled in his triumph, a perverse celebration of the transgression he had orchestrated.

Meanwhile, the first couple's newfound realization of their nudity sparked a frantic search for coverings, a tangible manifestation of their altered consciousness. It was not merely the fruit that was consumed, but the innocence that had once cloaked them, now irretrievably lost.

As the gravity of her deed sank in, Eve was struck by a profound and harrowing insight: through her actions, she had incurred an indelible stain—sin. This breach of trust placed her, and by extension humanity, in opposition to God's holiness.

The breach widened into a chasm, and the repercussions were swift and severe. Adam and Eve, once the cherished stewards of paradise, were exiled from the bounteous Garden of Eden, severed from the divine presence that had so lovingly shaped their existence.

Creations Lament and Promise

In the shadow of the fall, the flawless work of divine artistry, once teeming with life in perfect unison, took an irrevocable descent towards decay. The harmony that had characterized the relationship between God, humankind, and the divine council was now fractured, spiraling into a state of desolation. Earth, along with all its inhabitants, bore the weight of a profound curse.

Echoing throughout the ages, as if in a present state of mourning, creation itself appears to resonate with the distressing sentiments expressed in Romans 8:22: "For we know that the whole creation has been groaning together in the pains of childbirth up to the present time." Sin's corrosive influence severed the intimate closeness between humanity and the Divine, heralding an era of gradual degradation for the world we had known.

In Genesis 3:15, the narrative weaves both humankind and the evil divine into the fabric of this curse. An enmity is pronounced to endure through generations: "I will put hostility between you and the woman and between your offspring and hers. He will crush your head, and you will strike his heel." In this profound proclamation, the Divine articulates an inextricable link between humanity and the celestial adversary. It is a tangled knot of conflict, yet within the very fibers of this curse, there lies an embedded glimmer of eventual triumph and the beginning thread of redemption.

Once an impossibility, the tragedy has unfolded, and what was never intended to be has become our reality. As the heart of humanity has been marred, Jeremiah 17:9 casts a stark light upon our new nature: "The heart is deceitful above all things and beyond cure. Who can understand it?" The innate purity and goodness that once defined us have been supplanted by darkness and deceit.

Satan, once a mere specter in the divine narrative, has now assumed a chilling title: the ruler of this world. In his shadow, much of humanity has veered from the path intended for them, succumbing instead to the temptations and wiles that echo his rebellion.

Confronted with this grim inheritance—estrangement from the source of life—humankind finds itself poised on the brink of an abyss, an eternal demise. Yet hope is not extinguished, for within the pages of scripture runs a resilient thread, one that weaves through every text and tale: it is the story of God's redemptive love, a relentless quest to salvage the once unblemished bond between Creator and creation.

This narrative of salvation, reaching across time and testimony, forms the backbone of the Bible. It is a testament to divine mercy so profound that it seeks to offer humanity another path, a possibility of restoration beyond the bleak prospect of eternal death—a harbinger of grace in the midst of our self-made desolation.

The Shadow of Sin

Scripture repeatedly warns us that the wages of sin are far-reaching and grave, encompassing death and a cascade of destructive outcomes. It permeates the tapestry of our existence, its repercussions manifesting in various dimensions of our daily lives. The stems of sin entangle themselves in three critical areas that shape our human experience: physical ailments, emotional turmoil, and spiritual emptiness.

Physical ailments serve as tangible reminders of the broken state of our world, a direct contrast to the pristine health that once flourished. Emotional dysfunctions disrupt our innate capacity for harmony and connection, leaving us with a pervasive sense of imbalance. Spiritual emptiness, perhaps the most profound of these afflictions, echoes the ultimate disconnection from our Creator, a yearning for a wholeness that seems ever elusive in the wake of our transgressions.

Sin creates an intrinsic discord between God and us, one that not only strains our spiritual well-being but can also manifest in physical afflictions. The internal conflict bred by sin often surfaces as health issues, exerting a harmful toll upon our bodies. Each struggle with sin, whether it's an eating disorder, substance abuse, or other self-destructive habits, carries the potential to disrupt our physiological functions.

It can adversely impact blood pressure, interfere with restful sleep, or ravage the body in numerous ways dictated by our lifestyle choices. Engaging in physical sin disrupts the delicate balance intended for our well-being and hinders our ability to exist in harmony with God.

Scriptural wisdom cautions us that the broad and unchallenging path, while seemingly inviting, ultimately ushers us toward ruin. Notably, the peril of this path extends beyond mere physical demise—it carves out a void of emotional turmoil characterized by feelings of emptiness, despair, and profound disconnection. Many tread this path in search of emotional fulfillment, lured by the false promise that sin can satisfy the depths of their yearnings.

Regrettably, the allure of sinful pleasures is a mirage, incapable of providing the emotional sustenance it purports to offer. Emotional sin entrenches us in self-reliance and clouds our judgment, leading us to rationalize behaviors that misalign with our spiritual compass.

The aftermath of such transgressions can be a heavy heart mired in regret, the shadows of depression, and even the stark contemplation of self-harm. These are the harrowing emotional legacies of sin, leaving scars on the soul that reverberate long after the fleeting satisfaction has faded.

Spiritual Estrangement and Redemption

One of the gravest outcomes of sin that resonates universally is that of spiritual death. This widely acknowledged consequence reveals how sin severs the precious bond between the Divine and us, leading to profound spiritual disconnection. Beneath this surface understanding, we encounter the heartrending realizations of those who feel unbearably unworthy of any divine interaction due to their misdeeds. Burdened by such convictions, they abstain from forging or mending a relationship with God, convinced of their own unworthiness.

This chasm that sin has chiseled between the individual and God prompts introspection—many have pondered over the aching distance that has grown, questioning, "How did I become so estranged from God?" The choices made in isolation from God's wisdom fail to usher us into harmony with the Divine, and over time, this distance only intensifies.

Pause for a moment to envision the era predating the redemptive incarnation of Jesus Christ. How vast the chasm between humanity and God must have felt when a direct path to reconciliation was not yet revealed! Before the grace afforded through Jesus, a gulf of separation was all that humankind comprehended, with divine encounters few and far between—moments when God, in His sovereign initiative, reached across the divide.

Unreachable by our own devices, we stood robbed of the warm embrace of the true living God. This bleak outlook underscores the magnitude of the gift we have received through Jesus, who bridged the once-insurmountable divide, offering an enduring hope of reuniting with the Divine and experiencing His presence anew.

Misjudging our Missteps

In pondering our human deviations, I recall an insightful article from the Got Questions website where the writer highlighted a common, yet flawed, tendency among us: the inclination to downplay our imperfections. There's a pervasive hope that God's love will render Him lenient, that He will turn a blind eye to our minor infractions, lapses, and misguided acts.

We often categorize our small deceits—those little white lies—or rationalize slightly fudging our tax returns. We may try to dismiss the weight of taking something that isn't ours, or secretly indulging in pornography, as trivial. Following in Eve's footsteps, we engage in internal negotiations over our actions, assuring ourselves that such misdemeanors surely don't merit the stern consequence of death, do they?

In musing thus, we not only echo Eve's ancient rationalization but also misjudge the impact of our sins—no matter how seemingly insignificant—on our spiritual integrity and our relationship with God. At its core, sin, whether perceived as major or minor, is an affront to the divine order, an aberration in the face of purity.

It's a fundamental misalignment with the nature of God, who, in His boundless love, is also the incarnation of holiness—so much so that He stands in stark opposition to all forms of evil. The prophet Habakkuk articulates this divine attribute with clarity: *"Your eyes are too pure to look on evil; you cannot tolerate wrongdoing"* (Habakkuk 1:13).

It's a misconception that God might overlook our sins; rather, His very essence dictates a response to sin. The warning conveyed in Numbers 32:23, *"be sure your sin will find you out,"* emphasizes the certainty with which our misdeeds demand attention. None can be hidden or minimized; all are significant in the sight of the Divine.

This truth extends to the concealed sins, those we guard within our innermost selves, veiled from human eyes but transparent to God. Scripture reveals an unvarnished truth in Hebrews 4:13: *"Nothing in all creation is hidden from*

*God's sight. Everything is uncovered and laid bare before the
eyes of Him to whom we must give account."*

It serves as a solemn reminder of our ultimate accountability, that one day everything—the seen and unseen, the
acknowledged and denied—will be manifested in the presence of God.

The Inevitability of Sin's Outcome

The apostle Paul underscores a principle that reverberates
through time and conscience alike: our actions have inevitable and corresponding repercussions. He cautions us with
unambiguous firmness, *"Do not be deceived: God cannot be
mocked. A man reaps what he sows"* (Galatians 6:7). Here,
Paul lays bare the stark reality that sin engenders consequences, dismissing any notion that divine justice may be
circumvented.

Elaborating on the dire trajectory of choosing sin, he
expounds, *"The one who sows to please his sinful nature,
from that nature will reap destruction"* (Galatians 6:8). The
term "sinful nature" depicts the aspect of humanity that is
untransformed and crude, pursuing gratification without a
thought to the moral decline.

Despite its hollow assurances of satisfaction, succumbing
to this base self is a path that leads impossibly to one end—
destruction. It is a destructive harvest, born from the seeds
of transgression, providing sobering clarity that fulfillment
sought in rebellion against divine order is ultimately a pursuit of ruin.

Paul painted a vivid contrast for the Galatian believers, highlighting the divergence between the sinful nature and the realm of the Spirit. *"The sinful nature desires what is contrary to the Spirit, and the Spirit what is contrary to the sinful nature. They are in conflict with each other..."* (Galatians 5:17). This dichotomy he describes speaks to the perpetual clash within the human heart—a tug-of-war between impulses leading towards degradation and those aspiring to divine.

Diving deeper, Paul delineates the depraved acts birthed by our baser instincts, cautioning that such behaviors carry dire, eternal ramifications: *"Those who live like this will not inherit the kingdom of God"* (Galatians 5:19-21).

A life steeped in vice and sinfulness not only tarnishes one's earthly existence, seeding ruin amidst fleeting pleasures but also jeopardizes the prospect of life everlasting. It is a sobering reminder that the choices we make under the sway of sinful pursuits have the power to close the door on our heavenly inheritance.

Redemption Restored

Those well-versed in the Bible recognize the core narrative that has been unwound since the time of the ancient past: God's relentless pursuit of humanity. Despite every setback and transgression, His unwavering blueprint for fellowship with His creation endures, culminating in the person and work of Jesus Christ and His resurrection.

Paul captures this redemption arc in Romans 5:18-19, explaining the profound symmetry in humanity's spiritual journey: *"Just as one trespass resulted in condemnation for all people, so also one righteous act resulted in justification and life for all people.*

For just as through the disobedience of the one man the many were made sinners, so also through the obedience of the one man, the many will be made righteous." This passage illuminates the transformative power of Christ's sacrifice and triumph over death.

The crucifixion and resurrection of Jesus represent the ultimate act of submission to the Divine will—a pivotal moment that reopens the gateway to God's presence for us. Through Jesus' obedience, we are liberated from the chains of sin and granted the privilege to enter into the holy communion that was once severed, now restored through grace.

The initial rebellion in Eden marked humanity's critical departure from the Divine plan, a transgression so profound that only the intervention of Jesus could mend it. With sin's advent, the specter of death cast a shadow across creation, its stark finality threatening an unending rift between humans and God.

Yet, with emergence from the darkness of the tomb, Jesus bore the dawn of restoration. His resurrection was not merely an act of divine power but the herald of eternal life for all who would embrace it.

In defeating the grave, Jesus lifted the curse of death that had befallen mankind, extending an offer rich with Grace and Mercy—an invitation to reclaim the destiny once lost to sin.

This narrative unfolds into the Easter story that has imprinted itself upon the hearts of believers throughout the ages. It is the story of humankind's initial, grand rebellion against the Divine—a cataclysmic severance that only the Son could rectify. In His ultimate sacrifice and triumphant resurrection, Jesus restored the primordial harmony that predated our fall, reestablishing the divine order that was intended from the beginning.

A Scene of Divine Judgment

As we draw this chapter to a close, picture yourself amidst a solemn courtroom, with the Divine presiding as Judge. The air is heavy with the gravity of the trial – you stand in the dock, the accused, facing allegations of transgressions against God Himself. The growing list sits before you, an indictment of your soul's misdeeds, and in the silence of your own heart, you recognize your undeniable guilt.

Among the charges, a few echo within you, resonating with a disquieting clarity: you have harbored murder in your heart, not against one, but a multitude. Repeated lies, varied in magnitude, weave through your history. But above all, it is the accusation of blaspheming against God that pierces you the deepest, a wound of words for which you yearn forgiveness.

The moment of reckoning arrives. As you stand vulnerable before the bench, the weight of expectation presses down. You know what the declaration will be. And as the Judge pronounces 'Guilty', the word reverberates throughout the chamber. There is no surprise, no gasp, for you are intimately acquainted with the truth of your actions. The verdict, though anticipated, resounds with the finality of judgment.

You are acutely aware of the harsh penalty prescribed for your crimes—an eternity in hell, a realm of gnashing teeth and unquenchable thirst, a fate far beyond any mortal's worst nightmare. The understanding of what awaits fills you with indescribable dread, and as tears begin to blur your vision, a sense of impending torment grips your very essence.

In the depths of despair, a voice breaks through—resonant, authoritative, merciful. The Judge declares, "Mercy!" Confusion permeates your thoughts. "Mercy?" you wonder in disbelief. Your eyes lift, seeking confirmation, and in this moment of unbelief, your gaze meets His—the one who stands in your defense.

Jesus, your advocate, affirms with unwavering certainty, "It is true." The weight of your sins, once a shackle upon your soul, is lifted. "Your sins are forgiven; you will live with me in heaven for all eternity," He proclaims.

In an instant, joy unbounded floods your being; a spiritual exultation the likes of which you've never known. You can hardly fathom the reality: you have been liberated, your sin's chains shattered. As Jesus embraces you, His words, "Well done, good and faithful servant," echo within, not just as a commendation but as a welcome into a new, everlasting life of freedom.

Following the profound forgiveness pronounced by Jesus, an astonishing transformation unfolds. The Judge rises from His seat, not in a gesture of departure, but to approach you. With an all-encompassing warmth, He embraces you, not only as a sovereign judge but as a loving Father intent on bestowing further acts of kindness.

"I also want to give you Grace," He declares, His voice brimming with compassion. "While you navigate the earthly journey, this gift shall be yours freely. I desire to sustain you, to endow you with the means to live righteously."

He assures you, "My grace is sufficient for you, for it enabled My Son to exemplify a holy life amidst mortal toils. Let this grace be your stronghold. When your heart harbors dark thoughts, when evil intent whispers, my grace will steer you towards forgiveness and peace. When falsehoods tempt you, it's my grace that will empower your honesty. In the clutches of fear, it will be my grace that offers comfort.

The Judge—God Himself—extends to you an invitation to partake in His endless generosity. "I desire to bless you in abundance, to grant you access to the wealth of my kingdom, that you may flourish under my provident care." This grace is a fountain of strength and guidance, assuring you never have to face your trials alone.

As the magnitude of the Judge's words sank in, a fresh surge of tears blurred your vision—these, however, were tears of astonishment. A profound rush of emotion swept over you, rendering you speechless, your knees giving way to the overwhelming sense of underserved favor that blanketed you. There, in your deepest humility, you knew beyond doubt that none of this extraordinary mercy was earned.

Gently, Jesus stooped, His hands reaching out to lift you from your position of awe. "What I accomplished on the cross," He reassured you, "is the source of all these blessings. The moment you entrusted your life to Me, mercy and grace were bestowed upon you in full measure."

His voice carried the weight of absolute truth, "My love for you is without flaw, my yearning for communion with you knows no end." With a solemn yet tender exhortation, He blessed you, "Be blessed, my child, and embrace the liberty I have graciously granted." Under His boundless love, you were called to rise and step into the expanse of freedom that Christ had secured—freedom that was yours to hold forever.

The Unfathomable Gift

As I pen these words, a swell of emotion rises within me, and tears blur the ink on the page. I pause, reflecting on the immeasurable love and sacrifice Jesus has borne on my behalf, and a voice within me whispers, "This is the greatest news ever." In quiet contemplation, I sit with the enormity of all that has been done for me, when a realization dawns— there is more depth to this story yet to be explored.

We acknowledge the bitter truth: our sins forge the barrier that stands between us and communion with Jesus. And more so, we recognize the adversary's opportunistic nature. Satan seizes upon our propensity to sin, endeavoring at every turn to obstruct the sublime architecture of God's redemptive plan—a plan that has been unfolding since the dawn of creation.

As we prepare to delve into the subsequent acts of defiance, let us first take stock of Satan's persistent attempts to derail the divine blueprint for our salvation. In doing so, we are reminded of God's unwavering fidelity to us, the lengths to which He has gone, and continues to go, countering every twist and turn of the enemy's schemes. It is within this cosmic contest that the steadfast love of God shines brightest, reassuring us that no force can ever quench His determination to restore us to Himself.

Chapter 7

Grand Hall of Divine Words

Narrative:

In this chapter, you will be guided to a magnificent hall where you will come face-to-face with God. He will share His words about how He has safeguarded the path of redemption. This is crucial for us to understand as it exemplifies God's unwavering pursuit of humanity in this extraordinary divine tale of love.

Opening Scene:

The vast chamber unfurls with celestial grandeur, an expanse more immense than the greatest earthly libraries. Towering shelves, stretching endlessly upward into a twilight haze, cradle what seem to be countless shimmering volumes radiating with a supernatural glow.

You stand bewildered in the center of the room, the air thick with the scent of ancient parchment and echoes of sacred whispers. Your eyes struggle to comprehend the space around you, a sanctum of divine dialogue where the fabric of reality is woven with words of power and purpose.

You are but a lone sojourner amidst the extremely delicate archives, unsure of your own arrival. Yet, in this hallowed repository of the Almighty's utterances, there is a profound understanding of being exactly where you are meant to be—a witness to the story of redemption, written from before the foundation of the world.

You pace with hesitant steps, guided by an inexplicable pull within the depths of your spirit, through rows of pulsating stories—each echo a testimony of the conversations held within the divine council, spanning the ages across heavens and earth.

The scene shifts before you, cascading through the annals of time: Cain and Abel, offerings laid bare upon the earth. Genesis 4:4-5 flickers in the air, words portraying God's pleasure in Abel's sacrifice but showing no favor for Cain's.

The serenity shatters as you perceive the seismic shift in Cain's heart, the Divine Script painting every brushstroke of his internal battle in real-time. The air turns cold and you shiver as you read the invisible ink, a subtext revealing how, in Cain's resentment, the serpent found his lair. Genesis 4:7 whispers, "Sin is crouching at your door; it desires to have you, but you must rule over it."

Yet Cain falls not to sin alone; his downfall is one of blood and earth, brother slaying brother, severing the lineage that was to carry the promise. You feel a swell of mourning, heartache etched within the celestial parchment that narrates the fracture of the divine narrative intended since Eden—the disruption of redemption's flow.

As Man Sins, God Adjusts

Transitioning scenes crystallize and refocus on a heartened note with the advent of Seth—triumph emerging from tragedy. Words coalesce into assurance, a covenant renewal as the lineage finds breath anew. Genesis 4:25, a verse bearing hope, rests before your eyes, glowing with delicate light:

"For God has appointed another seed for me instead of Abel, whom Cain killed."

You feel the Divine Presence all around as if God Himself is whispering into the very essence of this moment. In Seth's birth, God's narrative of salvation endures, a tapestry of mercy and grace that cannot be torn asunder by even the most violent acts of rebellion or sin. You sense both, the gravity and the grace of the Lord's plan unfolding as you watch Seth's line carry forward the promise through the ages.

The tale continues before your eyes, Genesis 5:1-32 unveils before you, recounting the generations, a genealogy from Adam through Seth, a lineage traced with divine precision. With each name, hope reverberates, an echo of God's unwavering commitment to rescue His creation. Here, amidst the annals of human history, you see the preparations for a King, a lineage shielded from the enemy's malice.

At the edge of your vision, the shadow of the adversary slithers, a reminder of the ever-present spiritual warfare. Yet even as Satan conspires, the sovereignty and wisdom of God appear conspicuously insurmountable. Psalms 2:1-4 speaks from a hidden corner, an ancient protest against the futility of the enemy's plotting, and assurance of the Lord's derision toward such vain schemes.

No longer seeing but hearing, Noah's Covenant

As you stand amid the archives of eternity, books pulsating with the living breath of God's spoken history. In the wonder of this moment, a scroll unfurls, swirls of celestial ink drawing forth the portrait of a pre-flood world drowning in its iniquity.

Your eyes land upon the lines of Genesis 9:1-17, where the words shimmer as the Noahic Covenant is established. A vision of NOAH, a righteous man among the corruption, working tirelessly on the ark amidst the ridicule of a fallen world. As the floodwaters recede, representing divine judgment and mercy, you hear GOD words in a soft, thunderous tone say *"I establish My covenant with you: Never again will there be a flood to destroy the earth."* I have defeated Satan's attempt to crush out my grand plan.

Suddenly, A magnificent RAINBOW arises inside this grand room, God's promise ascending through the mist, defying the shadow that sought to erase humanity's redemption.

As you tread further, the path leads you to a section marked by a warm glow, the ambiance shifts to a comfort that transcends human understanding. Here, inscribed upon these heavenly scrolls, you see another covenant, another promise in Genesis 12:1-3, as God speaks to Abraham:

> *"I will make you into a great nation, and I will bless you; I will make your name great, and you will be a blessing. I will bless those who bless you, and whoever curses you I will curse, and all peoples on earth will be blessed through you."*

And so, it is clear—in this grand room where eternity kisses the temporal—it is the unwavering voice of God that weaves through the chaos, persistently scripting a love story with humanity, a story of redemption that no force of darkness can thwart. Your mind struggles to grasp the weight of this revelation, yet your spirit understands: the words spoken here outlive time itself.

Moses Covenant

Out-of-nowhere A MOUNTAIN materializes, Sinai, surrounded by fire and smoke. Amid the peals of thunder, Moses descends with stone tablets, the Law etched by the finger of God. The Mosaic Covenant resonates through the valley, binding blessings to obedience. Yet as Moses looks upon the Golden Calf, the accuser sneers, anticipating the destruction of the chosen ones.

As your touch grazes the volumes, the very voice of God fills the cavernous Hall, golden and pure, resonating with the sadness and patience of the ages. It's as if the thoughts of the Almighty are made audible, echoing throughout the endless rows of divine records.

GOD with a thunderous, yet a tone of lament says, "Satan sowed seeds of fear among my children, engendering worry. Their practices strayed far from my perfect will, exhibiting hearts not fully yielded to my guidance. Discord was the fruit of their incomplete surrender."

A new scene paints itself in spectral light, an illustrative re-enactment of the Israelites encamped at the base of Mount Sinai, teetering between reverence and rebellion.

GOD gravely, tinged with exasperation says, "The adversary exploited their resistance, their half-hearted allegiance casting shadows of division. My righteous wrath blazed against their folly, their utter refusal to grasp the breadth of my love and purpose. A cleaner slate tempted me, beckoning a fresh genesis for humanity"...

The Hall shivers with the weight of impending judgment, a worldly reset hanging by a divine thread.

Then GOD softened, reflecting on mercy said, "But within Moses' faith ember glowed fiercely; his steadfastness stayed my hand. For his sake, for the continuance of the covenant that leads to Jesus, I persevered with this stiff-necked people."

The floor itself trembles as you move to touch upon the pages describing the forty-year odyssey in the wilderness—a generation passing, waiting for renewal and entry into a land sworn by God to their forebears.

GOD with finality, tinged with hope says, "It became necessary to refine them through trials and time. Only after the generation of doubt had yielded to dust did I shepherd the faithful remnant toward the very borders of the promise—a land flowing with milk and honey, a tangible embodiment of the covenant pledged to Abraham."

The Israelites now stand on the brink, peering across the Jordan as whispers of the past and future intermingle— legacies left to rest in the desert sands while hope beckons from the fertile hills before them.

You, a silent observer of this great tapestry, feel the gravity of God's eternal plan—a narrative unceasing, even when challenged by sin's chaos and Satan's schemes. The Hall stands as a testament to God's love for all humanity.

Joshua Leads the People

A BIBLICAL collection of memories unveils, depicting a whisper of God's voice to Joshua in Joshua 1:2-9, instilling courage and the call to be strong and of good heart. In the divine presence, Joshua ascends from apprentice to leader, imbued with the spirit befitting Moses' successor.

GOD encouraging but emboldening says, As Moses lifted his hands to part the sea, so Joshua lifted his feet to cross the Jordan. Both acts are threads of the same narrative— my sovereignty over creation, and my faithfulness to the covenant.

God then shows you how, even as Joshua takes up the mantle, the adversary, the serpent of old, weaves a new tapestry of terror among the tribes. Spies return with news of giants in the land of Canaan, the descendants of Anak, whose stature seemed to rival the cedars of Lebanon (Numbers 13:28-33).

GOD consoling yet overpowering says Yet, my covenant transcends the giants of the earth. In the land where they dwell, even there my promise looms larger. My servant Caleb spoke against the tide of fear, noting that the land they spied out was exceedingly good.

A flickering scene showcases the Israelites' tremulous hearts, succumbing to fear, a dread sown by the adversary in the hope of thwarting their destiny while stopping God's grand plan of redemption.

GOD resentful, yet resolute says, Satan's strategy remained unchanged—spread fear and foster disbelief among my children. But did I not promise to be with them as I was with Moses? Do I not command the day and constrain the night?

The delicate scene evolves, shifting to a depiction of Joshua and the Israelites mustering their faith, courage crystallizing amidst the shadow of dread. Each tenuous step into Canaan is met with God's unshaken fidelity, pushing back the woeful cloud cast by Satan's ploys. God declared that He would not permit them to fail, even though He would grant them the freedom to willingly submit to His instructions. Despite their failure to fully heed Him, He was pleased with Joshua.

King David Covenant

As you linger within the spiritual confines of the Hall, the victories of Joshua wane, giving way to the era of judges and, eventually, a united monarchy under a young shepherd king, David.

GOD affectionately said, David, a man after my own heart, ascended to the throne. Through him, I desired to establish an everlasting kingdom, for the scepter shall not depart from Judah, nor the ruler's staff from between his feet, until He to whom it belongs shall come.

The annals around you illuminate the narrative of 2 Samuel 7:12-16, where God promises David that His house, His kingdom, shall endure forever. This covenant, the Davidic Covenant, underlies the assurance of a Messiah—a King of kings—whose rule would surpass the bounds of time.

The Hall quivers as a shadow stirs from within the text— glimpses of Satan devising the derailment of David's line- age, exploiting human failures, and sowing discord within the royal family. Bathsheba, Uriah, Absalom, and Tamar— are all pawns in the chessboard of the adversary.

GOD soberly, with omnipotent wisdom, says, "The enemy weaved his scheme into the sinew of David's house, inflam- ing desires, instigating murder, inciting rebellion. Satan be- lieved that by fracturing the harmony of David's family, the sovereign line would be severed, the covenant nullified."

Yet, you perceive that within the narrative an unrelenting thread of grace arises. Despite David's own transgressions, despite a kingdom riven by intrigue and betrayal, God's promises remain irrevocable. The divine response echoes through the ages, confirming redemption through punishment and forgiveness rather than annihilation.

GOD firmly, with mercy unfathomable says, "My mercy triumphed judgment. With every sin, with every sorrow, my covenant stood as a beacon, never to be extinguished. For from the stump of Jesse, a shoot would emerge—a branch that would bear fruit for all eternity."

The rich tapestries depicting David's reign suddenly fade, as you are drawn further along the Hall. Despite myriad attempts by the forces of darkness to corrupt, divide, and conquer, God's unfailing covenant with David endures, a token of the steadfast love that stretches beyond the stars.

God's Next Chapter after David

Now you are deeply entrenched in the divine narrative, as you watch a timespan of the kings unfold. Shelves and scrolls pulse with the spectral history of Israel's monarchy—as things move back and forth between faithfulness and folly, with many of David's descendants straying from God's laws.

GODS' sorrow knit with steadfast resolve says, "My people, whom I brought forth from bondage, found themselves ensnared by the very sins from which I sought to liberate them. Idolatry blighted the land, and justice was twisted by mischief. Yet through the tempests of their defiance, I preserved a remnant loyal to David's throne."

As you observe how, despite pervasive corruption, divine providence shields the seed of David. From Solomon's splendor to the division of the kingdom, through the tumultuous reigns of Ahab and Jezebel, Hezekiah's reform, and Josiah's rediscovery of the Law, the sequence of succession remains unbroken.

Babylon Captivity

A chilling vision then reveals the advent of Babylonian captivity. Jerusalem falls, the temple is destroyed, and the line of kings is seemingly severed as the people of Judah are led away into exile. Their conquerors intend it a death blow for the Davidic Covenant, a dark hope fostered by Satan to see Israel's holy fire doused.

GOD a voice that shapes the course of nations says, "In their exile, though they dwelt in a foreign land, my eyes never departed from them. My warnings through the prophets were crystal clear—judgment was assured, yet so was restoration. For my promises are not bound by place, nor thwarted by powers or principalities."

Amidst visions of the exiles' plight, you see a hope humanized in figures like Daniel, Esther, and Nehemiah—beacons of faith who, even in oppression, cling to the God of their forefathers.

GOD with dignified assurance, says, "Even in the darkest night of their despair, the royal lineage lay dormant, like embers under ash awaiting the breath to kindle them afresh.

As I was with Daniel in the lions' den, so I was with the line of David, guarding it against the ravenous jaws of oblivion."

Prophets to Silence to Jesus

Transitioning through the Hall of Words, prophetic scrolls such as Jeremiah and Isaiah cast light on a future king, a servant, one to be cut off yet usher in an age of redemption, a cornerstone of salvation who would reconcile my creation unto myself.

It is the silence of prophets who have spoken their final words, their scrolls ending with promises not yet ful-filled—a divine interlude of 400 years takes place before the promised Messiah's entrance.

GOD's voice echoing through the silence says, "Across centuries of waiting, the whisper of my voice became a stillness in the hearts of my people. Seers and prophets gave way to a quiet expectancy, an anticipation for the One who was to come."

You can almost feel the adversary's restless energy during this silence, Satan's vain efforts to smother hope and cloud vision now amplified amidst the quiet. Dynasties rise and fall, empires set the stage, and yet the thread of redemption weaves its way through time, untouchable, unbreakable.

GOD's voice imbued with immutable intent says, "My word, once spoken, continues to echo even when human lips fall silent. My promises are self-sustaining, ignited by my own will to bring them to fruition." The enemy believed that silence could kill the promise, but it only served to underscore its certainty, its proximity.

In the stillness of the Hall, you discern the subtle preparations being made. Even as the people of God live out their lives under the rule of empires—Persian, Greek, and Roman—each geopolitical shift, each cultural exchange, is part of a divine choreography leading to the fullness of time.

GOD's voice of an artist putting the final touches to a masterpiece says, Satan's shadow moved through the motives of kingdoms, through broken covenants and oppressed peoples. Yet unknowingly, these very movements laid the foundations for the incarnate Word to enter the world at the appointed hour.

The Birth of Jesus

The silence in the Hall gives way to a soft melody, the herald of a newborn's cry from the town of Bethlehem, and the stirring of angels' voices announcing the good news that would cause great joy for all the people.

GOD's voice warming with joy says, out of the silence shall emerge the quiet stirrings of a virgin's courage, the humble birthplace of a king, and the arrival of shepherds at the cradle of divinity. The thread of redemption, carried through generations, now woven into flesh—the Living Word, the fulfillment of all I have spoken. In this child, my Son, the divine and human are inseparably joined, a tapestry of heaven and earth stitched together in a manger. He is the dawn of grace, the promised Seed, the One through whom all nations shall be blessed.

GOD's voice overflowing with love says, Satan's relentless quest to sever the cord of redemption has been in vain, for in this moment, the Word made flesh embodies the unquenchable light of hope. This child, Jesus, shall grow to be the bridge over chasms of sin and death, the doorway to eternal communion between God and man.

Path of Redemption Shines Bright

You are embraced by the gentle warmth of this revelation, as you look upon a vision unfolding within the Hall. Mary, a portrait of divine strength and tenderness; Joseph, the embodiment of protective faithfulness; and above all, Jesus—God with us.

GOD gently whispers as the vision fades, "Thus, my story of redemption, woven throughout the ages, comes to breathe and walk among you, full of grace and truth. Through Him, my covenant is renewed, hope is restored, and the serpent's head is finally crushed."

Now realizing the magnitude of what you have witnessed within the Grand Hall of Divine Words, you step back. With a heart full of wonder, you now carry the profound truth that no span of silence, no scheme of darkness, can ever hinder the sovereign will of God. The silence has been broken, the Word has spoken, and the path to redemption shines brightly, leading all who will follow to everlasting life.

Now that we can clearly see the divine thread of redemption, we still need to uncover two more rebellions that Jesus reversed in His death, burial, and resurrection. In the above narrative, I intentionally left out the three grand rebellions with all three being a part of Satan's plan to stop the thread of His redemption.

In our next chapter, we will tackle another key mosaic piece in uncovering how the Divine watcher's sin was used by God to fulfill part of His Grand Plan.

The upcoming chapter will provide us with a deeper understanding of the situation, unveil the next action Jesus had to take to reverse the curse and shed light on a better understanding of our role in our movie's storyline.

Chapter 8

Divine Watchers Sin

Narrative:

As we venture into this chapter, we're about to trace our steps back to the dawn of biblical history, delving into the turbulent saga of the Watchers—a celestial rebellion that marked a pivotal chapter in the divine narrative.

To lay the groundwork for our exploration, let's look back into the foundational texts of Genesis. The pages of the Bible will serve as our guide, providing the framework and backdrop necessary to navigate the complexities of this chapter.

Through these ancient scriptures, we'll illuminate the contours of a story that has shaped the course of human understanding—setting the stage for the earthshaking events that have left their lasting mark on the fabric of spirituality and belief.

Genesis 6:1-4: *When man began to multiply on the face of the land and daughters were born to them, the sons of God saw that the daughters of man were attractive. And they took as their wives any they chose. Then the Lord said, "My Spirit shall not abide in[a] man forever, for he is flesh: his days shall be 120 years." The Nephilim were on the earth in those days, and also afterward, when the sons of God came into the daughters of man and they bore children to them. These were the mighty men who were of old, the men of renown.*

Opening Scene:

So, now that we have set the stage, let your imagination transport you to a realm where there are billions of people around you, a time before the great flood that swept the earth.

Visualize yourself amidst an innumerable throng, with the bustling masses having reached a staggering scale. Longevity is the norm, with lives stretching across eight or nine centuries, and flourishing families—each with upwards of 40 plus children—contributing to a dizzying rate of expansion.

Navigating through this ancient society, a distinct impression strikes you. The inhabitants give forth an air not of communal warmth but of brash arrogance and unchecked pride. You find a startling lack of moral compass, the absence of which stirs within you a sense of unease for your own welfare. Observing the chaos, the term 'out of control' feels like an understatement—there is a pervasive sense that these people are on an irreversible course toward calamity.

With a sense of dismay, you find yourself questioning the divine presence. "Where is God amidst this depravity?" you wonder. "Does He not see? Will He not act?" In this moment of doubt, a verse from Genesis 6:5 returns to you: *"The Lord saw how great the wickedness of the human race had become on the earth, and that every inclination of the thoughts of the human heart was only evil all the time."*

With this echo of ancient scripture, the stark reality of God's awareness surrounds you and hints at the impending intervention by the Divine to confront the unrelenting tide of human corruption.

The recall of this verse from Genesis stirred something profound within you; your heart ached as the gravity of God's observation became clear. The context it provided was shattering: the memories of a world awash with indifference to the divine. Amidst the populace, there was a startling absence of fear or reverence for God—virtues that had dissipated as though they had never been. It seemed to you that hope had forsaken these people entirely.

Yet, as you navigated this moral wilderness, fraught with a sense of desolation, an extraordinary encounter punctured the prevailing darkness. This individual you met—and you hesitated to use the term 'person' lightly—radiated an essence that set him apart from the rest, suggesting an origin beyond the earthly plane.

In his presence, the lines blurred, and you questioned if perhaps he were an otherworldly messenger, an angel cloaked in mortal guise, testimonial to the notion that even in the midst of pervasive depravity, the celestial had not wholly abandoned mankind.

The individual before you defied ordinary comprehension; his actions bore the unmistakable imprint of the supernatural. It was evident in the wonders he performed that his mission transcended the mere mortal coil—he had been divinely commissioned, tasked with shepherding wayward souls towards righteousness.

His intellect—a beacon in those primeval times—shone with a mastery of technology and science that far surpassed the understanding of his contemporaries. He imparted this secret knowledge, instructing the people in feats of remarkable consequence, ensuring that their actions would echo through the records of earthly history.

This mysterious figure, veiled in human form yet possessing the aura of celestial origins, commanded a profound respect. His integrity and purpose resonated deeply with the people, elevating him in their esteem beyond all others. In a world spiraling into chaos, he stood as a pillar of virtue, a veritable human angel whose presence heralded the possibility of redemption and enlightenment.

Good and Bad Beings

As time marched on, your path crossed with several beings of virtue—a rare assembly of good-hearted human angels amidst a tumultuous sea of iniquity. Their efforts to illuminate the path of righteousness seemed ceaseless, yet, despite their toil, the hearts of the people remained calloused to the very notion of virtue.

The taint of corruption persisted, unmitigated by the presence of these celestial guardians; the populace continued to indulge in profane and ignoble acts. It was as though the very concept of good remained an enigma, eternally elusive to their grasping minds.

However, the encounter with a decidedly evil figure casts a new light on this pervasive disregard for the divine. This unscrupulous human angel—a stark contrast to those who strived for holiness—ignited a troubling thought: Could this insidious presence be the catalyst for the people's irreverence? Could these entities, masquerading as agents of light, in fact, bear the blame for the abounding godlessness? It was a chilling consideration—one that suggested a hidden battle at play, a war for the soul of mankind waged within the shadows of their perception.

Encountering this new human angel, you witnessed feats of wonder similar to those performed by the previous celestial messengers. Yet, there was a noticeable difference— the air around this being was charged with a discomfort, their intentions shrouded not in desire to do good, but in designs that seemed far from virtuous. Unlike the others, whose deeds were pure, this one carried a reputation tinged with darkness, striking fear rather than awe into the hearts of those they encountered.

Questions began to swarm your mind. Could this figure be a renegade angel, straying from a righteous path? Had the earlier angel you admired merely been a more skillful deceiver, concealing their true motives behind a veil of feigned goodness? The uncertainty of it all stirred turmoil within you, and heavy grief settled over your spirit as you contemplated the plight of mankind.

Caught amidst heavenly beings with unfathomable agendas, humanity seemed ever more vulnerable, teetering on the brink of spiritual peril. This confusion deepened your sorrow, as you yearned for signs of clear, uncorrupted guidance for a race seemingly forsaken.

As the days unfolded and the tapestry of your experience grew richer, the realization that the realm of angels was a spectrum between righteousness and rebellion came into sharper focus. Among them were those known as the Watchers—soldiers per se assigned by the Most High to provide guidance and governance among the people of the earth.

With time, the saga of these celestial beings became well-known, a narrative woven into the very fabric of society. To many, the Watchers were more than mere heavenly diplomatic; they were respected as heroes, figures of grandeur and mystery whose actions sent ripples through human existence.

Their presence had become an integral part of the lore that shaped civilizations, with stories of their deeds, both noble and ignoble, igniting the imaginations and beliefs of all. Yet, amidst the flattery and fear they inspired, the stark line dividing the good from the insubordinate became an ever-present reminder of the celestial drama that played out on the earthly stage.

The Watchers Defiance

In sharp contrast to their heavenly mandate, the rebellious Watchers were drawn to mortal desires, particularly the allure of human women. Their presence was frequently accompanied by a throng of female admirers, an entourage that served as a testament to their earthly entanglements. In your deepest intuition, a sense of impropriety throbbed —the interactions seemed out of place with the exquisite nature of these beings, but their pursuits continued relentlessly, devoid of any appearance of guilt or second thought.

Fueled by impulsive lust, these fallen Watchers crossed the forbidden threshold, engaging in intimate relations with the women of earth. The unions that ensued were abnormal, blurring the lines between divine and human, and from this taboo intermingling, children were born.

These offspring were the offspring of both worlds, yet belonged wholly to neither, adding another complex layer to the unfolding human drama that you, as a witness, struggled to comprehend.

Watchers Bore Giants

The offspring borne from the unions of the rebellious Watchers and human women were beings of awe-inspiring stature —giants who inherited not only the formidable strength of their celestial lineage but also the astute intelligence imparted by their watcher heritage. These hybrid creatures, known as the Nephilim, straddled two worlds: half-human, and half-divine, yet belonging fully to neither.

Marked by their dual nature, the Nephilim bore the rebellion of their angelic forebears. They, alongside their divine ancestor, carved a path of defiance against Yahweh, influencing the masses to forsake dependence on their Creator.

Steering the people towards reliance on mortal strength and wisdom, they seeded a spirit of self-rule that sought to replace divine reverence with self-sufficiency, further unraveling the fabric of spiritual allegiance designed since creation.

The teachings imparted by the rebellious Watchers were lessons in self-reliance, crafting a narrative wherein human beings could thrive independently, detached from any aid or guidance from the Divine. The Nephilim, with their towering presence and uncommon wisdom, further emboldened this self-directed philosophy.

Amidst the unfolding human epic, it seemed the insurrectionist faction of Watchers eclipsed those who remained true to their heavenly charge—their influence pervasive, their numbers seemingly inexhaustible. The result was noticeable and chaotic: mankind, untethered from its spiritual moorings, spiraled into anarchy.

Through their actions and their offspring, these dissident Watchers shaped a world order defiant of divine sovereignty. Authority and dominion were no longer perceived as coming from God; instead, the emergent spirit celebrated the superiority of human and hybrid might over God's will, setting the stage for the tumult that would necessitate nothing less than a divine reckoning.

Noah's Call to Salvation

Having borne witness to the profound disorder brought on by divine rebellion, you found yourself returning to the celestial splendor of God's throne room. Amid the hallowed chambers, angelic elders spoke with grave urgency—whispers of judgment and renewal filled the air.

"The sons of God have transgressed against humanity," they lamented, "and the hour has come to champion Noah." Among the mire of depravity, Noah shone as a beacon of righteousness—a man whose life was steeped in the reverent fear and observance of Yahweh's commands.

With solemn resolve, the mandate was given: Noah would construct an ark, a vast vessel that would cradle the seeds of a new beginning amidst the coming flood. This ark would stand as a beacon of hope for Noah and his lineage, a sanctuary from the cleansing wrath of the floodwaters ordained to purge the world of its evils.

Together, the divine council and Yahweh declared their intention to not only eradicate the corruption that had saturated the earth but also to protect and replenish its innocence. A pair of each living creature would join Noah's ark in this divinely orchestrated exodus, ensuring that life's tapestry would be woven anew upon cleansed soil.

While the decree was stern, the justice behind it resonated with undeniable righteousness in your heart. There was no malice in this divine pronouncement, only an aching necessity fueled by boundless love—a divine sorrow for what had been lost, yet also a fervent hope for the potential of what was to be reborn.

The Cosmic Purpose of Christ's Resurrection

Narrative:

This transgression represents the second grand act of rebellion against the Divine—an act that necessitated Christ's descent from the celestial realms. Jesus' mission was clear: to counteract the curse, to mend the fractures brought on by this sin, and instill restoration where there had once been decay. While the Great Flood initiated God's grand plan to restore redemption, it was the resurrection of Jesus that brought this work to its glorious culmination.

In the coming chapters, I will unfold the tapestry of redemption, detailing the precise ways in which Jesus triumphed over these rebellions, and how through His life, death, and resurrection, He reestablished the covenant and reclaimed that which was lost. Through His acts of unfathomable grace, Jesus bridged the chasm between the divine and the fallen, offering a path to reconciliation and eternal life.

This significant act of rebellion—though less emphasized in traditional Easter narratives—deserves its place within the Easter story alongside the fall of Adam. While the sin of Adam often takes precedence in our churches and teachings, the transgression of the Watchers tends to be overlooked, obscured by its complexity and the mysteries that surround it.

As we progress, these narratives will be weaved together, offering clarity and insight into the full scope of redemption. By the final pages, the interconnectedness of these events, and their collective impact on our understanding of salvation, will be illuminated, providing a richer and more complete portrait of the divine plan fulfilled through Jesus.

The depths of human depravity, coupled with the Watchers' rebellion, culminated in an event of truly cataclysmic proportions—God's decision to cleanse the earth with the flood. Such a radical measure underscores the gravity of the situation; yet, it also highlights God's profound love for mankind—a love so great that it compels Him to undertake extraordinary actions to realign the broken fellowship between humanity and Himself.

When we turn to chapter 11, we're confronted with the uncomfortable truth that humanity's fresh start in the post-flood world was short-lived. The construction and subsequent downfall of the Tower of Babel serve as a reminder of humanity's recurrent drift toward self-reliance and estrangement from the Divine.

This swing between alienation and reconciliation is a recurring motif throughout the scriptures. But, before we can proceed to that chapter, we must first look deeper into the "Sons of God" and the "Nephilim" in the next two chapters.

Chapter 9

The Sons of God - Watchers

Narrative:

With the stage set in the previous chapter, it's time to dive deeper into the origins of the story we've begun to unravel. To comprehensively understand the narrative we're exploring, let's return to the foundational source—Genesis 6:1-4.

By revisiting these verses that provide a glimpse into the early days of humanity's journey, we will carefully deconstruct and interpret the story. From this point, we'll embark on an in-depth examination of the events, piecing together the complex mosaic of information that has informed our discussion so far.

Genesis 6:1-4 When man began to multiply on the face of the land and daughters were born to them, the sons of God saw that the daughters of man were attractive. And they took as their wives any they chose. Then the Lord said, "My Spirit shall not abide in man forever, for he is flesh: his days shall be 120 years." The Nephilim were on the earth in those days, and also afterward, when the sons of God came in to the daughters of man and they bore children to them. These were the mighty men who were of old, the men of renown.

Over time, the verses in Genesis 6:1-4 have sparked considerable debate among scholars, theologians, and believers alike. As we dissect these passages, I aim to provide context and clarity to the discussion at hand. To open, I want to clarify my own interpretation: I view the term "sons of God" as referring to the Watchers, aligning them with the concept of biblical angels. This is distinct from the role of the 24 elders described in the previous chapter.

The term "Watchers" emerges both in singular and plural forms in the Book of Daniel, which is a point I will delve into shortly. These Watchers are said to have fathered offspring known as 'Nephilim'—translated by many as 'giants' and mentioned specifically in the four verses of Genesis 6:1-4. Consistent with prior explanations, I perceive the Nephilim as hybrids: part human, part angel, a union shrouded in mystery and laden with implications from a theological perspective.

Historical Context

Providing historical context, there are three primary interpretations surrounding the hard-to-understand "sons of

God" mentioned in Genesis 6:2 and 6:4. These interpretations have evolved over time, with each offering a distinct perspective on the identity and nature of these beings. Two of these theories cast "the sons of God" as human lineages, while the third says that they are of angelic descent.

The earliest documented interpretation is found within a fragment of the Dead Sea Scrolls, known as 4Q417. This ancient text presents the "sons of God" as descendants of Seth, the third son of Adam and Eve. It portrays these individuals as the ones who transgressed the divine ordination, thereby rebelling against God. This interpretation implicates the lineage of Seth in the turmoil leading up to the flood narrative—a significant point of departure from later interpretations that would arise.

The Sethite interpretation says that the "sons of God" referred to in Genesis were indeed the offspring of Seth, aligning with an earlier passage where Seth's descendants are described as those who began to "invoke the name of the LORD" (Genesis 4:25-26)—a reference to their initial faith in God.

However, according to this view, these faithful descendants strayed by allying themselves with the "daughters of Cain," who were considered unbelievers and unrighteous. This intermingling between the lineages of Seth and Cain represents their rebellious turning away from God.

Over the centuries, this Sethite interpretation has found favor among a majority within the Christian tradition. It presents a narrative of spiritual decline through unholy unions, a common theme throughout biblical texts. Despite its widespread acceptance, the Sethite interpretation is not without its challenges.

A question lingers: Why would the offspring of these unions be referred to as "giants," or Nephilim if the union was solely between human lineages? This anomaly seems incongruent with the expectation of human offspring, and for me, this discrepancy casts doubt upon the Sethite explanation, leading me to consider alternative interpretations of the Genesis account.

The second theory exploring the identity of "the sons of God" in Genesis 6:1-4 is known as the "royal tyrant interpretation." This view suggests that the term refers to influential rulers of the time—potentially once-faithful descendants of Seth or those from the line of Cain—who succumbed to spiritual decadence. These leaders, possibly demon-possessed, are thought to have amassed harems and engaged in selective breeding practices, aiming to create offspring that would enhance their dominion.

Kermit Zarley of Patheos reflects on the Hebrew word "took" (laqach) in Genesis 6:2, noting its connotation of taking "for oneself," potentially implying the exertion of force in these unions. Over several generations, the outcome of such strategic human breeding is proposed to have birthed the Nephilim—giants of renown who might have accomplished extraordinary feats, earning them legendary status. Their legacies are hypothesized to have inspired pagan myths, which later coalesced into the mythologies familiar to us today.

Nonetheless, I find it difficult to reconcile this interpretation with the notion of merely demon-possessed kings, rather than angels imbued with divine attributes. My reading of scripture suggests an alternative understanding—one that diverges from the royal tyrant interpretation and beckons towards a more celestial explanation of these "sons of God.

Interpreting the Sons of God in Genesis and Enoch

Finally, we turn to a perspective that resonates with many in both the Jewish and Christian traditions—myself included—known as "the fallen angel's interpretation" of the "sons of God" in Genesis 6:1-4. This interpretation identifies these "sons of God" as angels who engaged in forbidden sexual relations with human women; a union believed to have produced offspring known as the Nephilim—individuals of both human and angelic descent, described as giants.

Renowned scholars like Michael Heiser, along with many others, support this interpretation, viewing the Nephilim as the hybrid offspring of this extraordinary interaction. The most comprehensive ancient account aligning with the fallen angel's narrative is found in the Jewish, intertestamental, and non-canonical text of 1 Enoch, particularly in chapters 6 through 12.

While it does not directly quote Genesis 6:1-4, 1 Enoch vividly portrays a group of 200 "angels" who conspired to take an "oath"—described therein as a "curse"—committing to undertake "this great sin" (1 En 6:1-6) against the orders of Heaven.

The extensive detailing of this event in 1 Enoch lends significant weight to the fallen angel's concept, marking it as a widely acknowledged interpretation that offers a fascinating lens through which to view the mysterious narrative of the early chapters of Genesis.

During the Second Temple period, the fallen angel's interpretation was a widely held belief among the Jewish community. The esteemed philosopher Philo of Alexandria lent credibility to this view in his work "On the Giants."

In that text, he offers an interpretative paraphrase of Genesis 6:2, illustrating the narrative in these terms: "And when the angels of God saw the daughters of men that they were beautiful, they took unto themselves wives of all of them whom they chose." This rendition by Philo not only echoes the sentiments of the era but also serves to underscore the prevalence and acceptance of the fallen angel's narrative within ancient Jewish thought.

For those seeking a scholarly exploration of this subject, Michael Heiser's "The Unseen Realm" comes highly recommended. Heiser offers a meticulously researched and peer-reviewed examination, providing expansive context that enriches comprehension of the matters at hand. His work illuminates the historical and theological complexities surrounding the Watchers and the Nephilim with exceptional clarity.

As previously noted, much of the contemporary understanding of the Watchers and Nephilim is drawn from the apocalyptic Book of Enoch and the Book of Jubilees. These ancient texts provide extensive commentary on the narratives briefly touched upon in Genesis. However, before we delve into these sources, it's instructive to examine the Book of Daniel, chapter 4.

Book of Daniel Term for Watchers

In the Book of Daniel, the word "Watchers" emerges distinctively, presented across three passages that contribute a vital layer to the canonical tapestry detailing these celestial entities. These scriptural moments beckon for careful contemplation, poised to deepen our understanding of the divine order and its reverberations through the records of the human saga. Let's look into each of these pivotal instances:

In Daniel 4:13, the text narrates a revelatory vision: *"I saw in the visions of my head upon my bed, and behold, a watcher and a holy one came down from heaven."* This imagery introduces the motif of a "watcher" as a divine messenger, underlining the intersection between the celestial realm and mortal experience.

Further unfolding this theme, Daniel 4:17 recounts, *"This matter is by the decree of the watchers, and the demand by the word of the holy ones: to the intent that the living may know that the Most High rules in the kingdom of men, and gives it to whomsoever he will, and set up over it the basest of men."* Here, the watchers are depicted as agents of divine will, underscoring that sovereign authority ultimately rests with the Most High.

In the directive issued in Daniel 4:23, we read, "*And whereas the king saw a watcher and a holy one coming down from heaven, and saying, Hew the tree down, and destroy it; yet leave the stump of the roots thereof in the earth, even with a band of iron and bronze, in the tender grass of the field; and let it be wet with the dew of heaven, and let his portion be with the beasts of the field, till seven times pass over him.*" This pronouncement signifies the watchers' role in the execution of divine judgments, highlighting their function within God's administrative structure.

Through these scriptures, the identity and duties of the Watchers become increasingly discernible, framing them not merely as observers but active participants in the divine narrative—a narrative that intersects fatefully with the course of kingdoms and the lives of rulers within the human domain.

The Guardians from Above

Within the verses of Daniel, we discern a portrait of the Watchers depicted as celestial guardians—anointed with divine authority to enact the will of God on earth. Initially, I approached these verses with a cursory understanding, perceiving the Watchers as typical members of the angelic host, without recognizing their potential connection to the mysterious "sons of God" and the Nephilim mentioned in Genesis 6:1-4.

It was not until I delved into the additional texts—the Book of Enoch and the Book of Jubilees—that I gained a deeper insight into their identities. These ancient writings offer rich commentary on the nature and roles of the Watchers, bridging the gap between the sparse references in the canonical scriptures and a more expanded conceptualization of these divine beings.

Book of 1 Enoch and Jubilees align events of the Old Testament

The Book of Enoch and the Book of Jubilees offer invaluable insights that extend our understanding of the Watchers, providing not only background but also a chronology aligning with the events of the Old Testament. Through these texts, the actions and purposes of the Watchers are cast into sharper relief. To illustrate my point, let me draw from a selection of verses from both Enoch and Jubilees:

The role of the Watchers in interceding for humans is highlighted in 1 Enoch 15:2, shedding light on the notion from Daniel 4:13 that they served as mediators between God and man.

In Jubilees 4:6, the Watchers are tasked with guiding people on the correct path of life, observing their deeds, and reporting the good or evil they witness back to God.

The revelatory function of the Watchers becomes evident in 1 Enoch 60:11, where it is noted that they disclose divine secrets.

They are also seen as preparing for the judgment of both the righteous and wicked, as echoed in 1 Enoch 103:2-3, indicating their involvement in eschatological processes.

Lastly, the transference of knowledge and skills from the divine to the human realm is attributed to the Watchers in 1 Enoch 7:1 and 8:1ff, where they teach men various arts and sciences.

These passages enrich our understanding of the activities and significance of the Watchers within the broader tapestry of religious texts, making it clear of their multifaceted roles as divine ambassadors, educators, and intermediaries in the unfolding narrative of humanity's spiritual journey.

The Darker Side of the Watchers

The figures known as the Watchers appear in the texts of Enoch and Jubilees with a rather darker connotation, one entwined with the actions of Satan. To acknowledge these aspects, let's review the relevant passages:

The similarity of Enoch narrates a tale of deviation, where specific Watchers are seduced from their heavenly abode by the first two of the five Satans, as outlined in 69:4 and 54:6. Additionally, in a celestial revolt led by Satanail, Watchers from the fifth heaven are lured into rebellion against God. This same Satan is prophesied to serve as both accuser and tormentor of the fallen Watchers, as per Enoch 54:3, 5.

Other accounts describe the punishment of the fallen Watchers: some are confined within the second heaven, while others are expelled to earth. On earth, these Watchers engage with human women, resulting in the birth of the Nephilim, the giant offspring cited in Genesis 6. These events are further expanded upon in texts such as Jubilee 13:17-35 and the Testament of Reuben 5:6.

While these verses offer intriguing insights, a comprehensive analysis would require a more expansive discourse—not the directive of this current work. There are ample commentaries already in existence that look into these stories, offering explanations for the curious reader.

However, it is important to recognize how the information from Enoch and Jubilees intersects with the canonical accounts found in Genesis and Daniel. In the paragraphs to follow, I will reference additional excerpts from Enoch, but keep in mind that these barely skim the surface of the profound depths contained within these supplemental texts. To grasp the full magnitude of these themes, one's own exploration of the literature is paramount.

Unveiling the identity of the Watchers

The existence of the Watchers is an established phenomenon, and the evidentiary trail we've followed suggests a strong connection with the "sons of God" mentioned in Genesis 6:4. My exploration, enriched by the texts of Enoch and Jubilees, leads me to a singular conclusion: the Watchers are synonymous with the fallen angelic beings described in these ancient accounts.

One of the pillars reinforcing my belief is the reference we find in the biblical book of Jude, which offers a telling glimpse into the nature of these divine rebels:

"And the angels who did not keep their positions of author-ity but abandoned their proper dwelling—these he has kept in darkness, bound with everlasting chains for judgment on a great Day." - Jude 1:6

Further, the words of Enoch are echoed in Jude's epistle:

"It was also about these that Enoch, the seventh from Adam, prophesied, saying, 'Behold, the Lord comes with ten thousand of his holy ones, to execute judgment on all and to convict all the ungodly of all their deeds of ungodliness that they have committed in such an ungodly way, and of all the harsh things that ungodly sinners have spoken against him.'" - Jude 14–15 [Quoted from 1 Enoch 1:9]

Confronted with these verses, I find myself pondering: which angels could Jude be referring to? Those who once held positions of authority yet chose to forsake their ordained residence? My mind turns relentlessly to the Watchers—whose narrative aligns with this description of heavenly transgression.

In considering the passage from Jude alongside the com-plementary commentary provided by Enoch, it becomes clearer that no other scriptural account fits as elegantly with these verses as that of the Genesis 6 narrative. Herein, the tapestry of textual evidence weaves a coherent picture, positioning the Watchers as key figures in this plot of primordial descent and divine judgment.

The New Testament further corroborates the involvement of celestial beings in earthly matters, attesting to their vested interest in human affairs and even detailing their capacity to assume human form. Such insights are found in passages like 1 Peter 1:12 and Hebrews 13:2:

"This Good News has been preached to you by those in the power of the Holy Spirit sent from heaven. So wonderful is this that even the angels are keenly observing these events unfold." - 1 Peter 1:12, NLT

"Be not forgetful to entertain strangers: for thereby some have entertained angels unawares." - Hebrews 13:2

Moreover, throughout the Bible, there are multiple affirmations of the vigilance and guardianship offered by angels to humanity:

"The angel of the LORD encamps round about them that fear him, and delivers them." - Psalm 34:7

"Take heed that you despise not one of these little ones; for I say unto you, that in heaven their angels do always behold the face of my Father which is in heaven." - Matthew 18:10

Instances such as Peter's angelic release from prison (Acts 12:9–15) serve as testaments to angelic intervention and protection.

In contemporary times, as reflected within the Church, one could argue that God's intent remains that His truth should be professed to all nations, offering divine wisdom not only to rulers but all corners of authority.

This vision resonates with the historical role fulfilled by the Watchers prior to Christ's resurrection and aligns with an understanding of God's ongoing orchestration of earthly governance. These scriptural illustrations, therefore, could suggest a biblical foundation for the perceived missions of divine watchers in both the past and the present.

Watchers' Rebellion and the Onset of the Flood

The Book of Genesis presents us with a brief yet compelling backdrop to the great Biblical Flood—a cataclysmic event precipitating Noah's construction of the ark. A pivotal moment arises in Genesis 6:1-5, where the transgressions of the Watchers are hinted as a significant catalyst for divine intervention.

Genesis 6:5 particularly illuminates the dire state of humanity, noting, *"And God saw that the wickedness of man was great in the earth, and that every imagination of the thoughts of his heart was only evil continually."*

Faced with a creation engulfed in corruption, God perceived no alternative but to initiate a dramatic reset, fully aware that this measure was not a permanent solution. A greater redemption was anticipated, one that would ultimately necessitate the salvation mission of His Son.

The sin of the Watchers did not merely represent their own revolt; it was a catalyst for mankind's broader insurrection against their Creator. As humanity's depravity reached its highest point, influenced by the celestial beings' disobedience, the necessity for both the world's and the Watchers' judgments became undeniable. This storyline is not only subtly woven into the Biblical text but builds to its crescendo directly ahead of the divine verdict to cleanse the earth with water.

The Book of 1 Enoch, chapter 10, goes on to articulate the fate allotted to these renegade Watchers, detailing their divine judgment for the sin of fraternizing with mortal women. Such narratives, while expanding on the cryptic references of Genesis, offer a tapestry of insight into the profound ramifications of these heavenly breaches and their direct correlation to God's grievous yet righteous decree.

The Fate of the Fallen

In a miserable and hidden realm, the Watchers await their destiny, shackled beneath the earth as recounted in the texts of 1 Enoch. There, their judgment looms—a fate aligned with the decree pronounced on the post-Babel Watchers in Psalm 82:7, where death is the sentence. This verdict finds its elaboration within the notion of an annihilating blaze:

"And to Michael God said, 'Make known to Semyaza and the others who are with him, who fornicated with the women, that they will die together with them in all their defilement. When they have seen the destruction of their beloved ones, bind them for seventy generations underneath the rocks of the ground until the day of their judgment and of their consummation, until the eternal judgment is concluded.'" - 1 Enoch 10:11-15

This explicit portrayal continues:

"In those days they will lead them into the bottom of the fire—torment—locked up forever. When they will burn and die, those who collaborated with them will be bound from henceforth unto the end of all generations. Destroy all the souls of pleasure and the children of the Watchers, for they have trespassed against mankind." - 1 Enoch 10:11-15

"And then... Michael, Raphael, Gabriel, and Phanuel... will cast [the sinful Watchers] into the furnace of fire that is burning that day, so that the Lord of Spirits may take vengeance on them." - 1 Enoch 54:6

This daunting notion of a flaming furnace resonates with the teachings of Jesus, who, within his parables, uses the same imagery to depict the final judgment upon sinners and transgressors:

"The Son of Man will send his angels, and they will gather out of his kingdom all causes of sin and all law-breakers, and throw them into the fiery furnace..." - Matthew 13:41-42

Although the Matthewan account as mentioned earlier seemingly targets human sinners, it is a modest leap to infer that transgressive angels, who also kindle sin, may likewise face this fiery reprimand—especially since 1 Enoch invokes a similar fate for the Watchers.

This extended discourse on the Watchers is not a mere historical footnote but rather a reflection on the disruption of divine order—a motif initiated by God for humanity to govern as servant-rulers upon the earth, as envoys of His will, executing stewardship in alignment with His just and sovereign rule.

In the presence of God's glory, they were to mirror divine wisdom and authority, but the Watchers' fall represents a profound deviation from this ideal, signaling a cosmos in disarray and necessitating divine intervention to restore balance and uphold the sanctity of creation.

From Watchers to Kings

The journey to recover the lost vision of Eden involves the establishment of Israel and the anointing of King David—a precursor to the promised Messiah. The Watchers were originally tasked with overseeing humanity, to act as divine guardians preserving order amid potential chaos. Their duty was never to lead humanity astray with corrupt teachings or to engage in acts defiling the divine-human relationship.

Their transgression mandated a divine reset: the Great Flood. This cataclysm served to reorient the trajectory that God had set, a plan aiming to reunite humankind with the divine presence. The insurgency of the Watchers and the knowledge they imparted in their defiance permeate our history to this day, setting the stage for Christ's earthly mission to undo this ancient curse.

However, before we explore the redemptive thread of how Jesus's resurrection reversed the curse, our next chapter will delve into the enigma of the Nephilim. We will tackle lingering questions such as their survival of the Flood and their role within the overarching narrative of divine purpose. Stay with me. In the next chapter, I will reveal the second Grand Rebellion that Jesus' resurrection overturned. I promise that everything will become clearer in the following chapters.

Moreover, we will witness in the coming chapters God's direct intervention at the Tower of Babel—humankind's quest to reclaim Edenic bliss epitomized in their striving for purpose and contentment.

Deprived of divine guidance, this pursuit inevitably deviates towards sin and rebellion. The Tower of Babel narrative not only marks the beginning stages of civilizations as we recognize them but also illuminates the divine response of assigning nations their boundaries while temporarily withdrawing divine favor.

In the ensuing chapters, we shall see how this dispersal of nations and the segmentation of God's attention sets the scene for a more focused divine strategy—one that prepares the world for the ultimate reconciliation and fulfillment of God's plan for unity with His creation. But now, in Chapter 10, we will unravel the mystery of the Nephilim Giants.

Chapter 10

Unraveling the Mystery of the Nephilim Giants

Narrative:

In this chapter, we embark on a journey into the mystifying realm of the Nephilim giants, beings that remained a topic of intrigue long after the Great Flood. We will explore various perspectives on this subject, drawing insights from scholars and researchers who have studied this fascinating topic.

Furthermore, we will look into the significance of Joshua's campaign against the giants in the Promised Land and understand why it was a crucial thread moment in God's divine plan.

Opening Scene:

Imagine that you are playing the role of an archaeologist, fully immersed in the character's perspective. As you handle physical matters in search of bones, it also prompts you to consider the Bible in search of spiritual insight. You want to know how the ancient giants managed to survive the flood and what their purpose was.

As an archaeologist you can distinctly feel the sense of isolation that surrounds the archaeological site, weighing heavily upon you. The echoes of ancient chapters closed in the records of history reverberate through the ruins that lay before you. Where once there might have been the hum of a bustling city, now only silence and the wind's whistling through stone hallways remain.

It's within this stillness that you come upon the skeleton—a behemoth structure, sprawling across the excavation ground, its bones a testament to a form of life that defies conventional understanding. The skeletal remains promise stories of an age where myth intertwined with reality, where figures of colossal might roamed Earth, possibly ruling it or perhaps terrorizing it.

You can't help but wonder—who were these giants? Were they the Nephilim spoken of in the Bible and ancient texts like Enoch, the offspring of beings divine and mortal? Your mind races with thoughts of how they might have lived, the sound of their footsteps, the nature of their existence.

Hazael's Conquest of Gath

You and your fellow archaeologists have exclusively proven Hazael's conquest of Gath through the archaeological remains found at a site known as Tell es-Safi.

It has been explored since 1899, but after 1996 the site has been excavated by the Tell es-Safi/Gath Archaeological Project, directed by Aaron Maeir (an American-born, Israeli archaeologist and professor at Bar Ilan University).

Located halfway between Jerusalem and Ashkelon, Tell-es-Safi has been the subject of intensive, technologically advanced archaeological exploration. However, it was what was discovered beneath the destruction layer of Hazael that has caused quite the archaeological stir. For instance, The Times of Israel news outlet stated:

"Digging a little deeper [in 2019, archaeologists] found impressive remains that predate the settlement destroyed by Hazael in 830 BC ..." described as: "Super-sized remains of 'enormous' architecture and fortifications ..."

The Times article explains that the majority of Tell es-Safi's previously excavated areas were dated to the 10th and 9th centuries BC, and had very little evidence of fortifications. However, the newly excavated layer beneath dates to the 11th century, and stands in stark contrast to the layers above in terms of its massive architecture. This is the correct period for the biblical narrative in 1 Samuel 17, when the future King David slew the giant Goliath.

Professor Maeir stated for the record:

"For those scholars that accept that David was a historical figure—and I'm among them—the late 11th–, early 10th [centuries BC], the time of the earlier phase of the city of Gath, whose impressive remains were just found, is the time frame in which David existed. … If in fact David did confront an opponent in single combat, most often identified as Goliath, this would, more or less, be the time of this early Iron Age phase of the city of Gath … [the discovered archaeological remains] show that the buildings and the fortifications were very large, built with extremely large stones … of much larger dimensions than almost anything found in the Levant during this era.

In later layers at the site … the ancient architects used half-meter-long (1.6 foot) stones. In the 'Goliath layer,' the blocks measure between one and two meters (roughly 3.2–6.5 feet)."4,6

In Quest of the Ancient

Driven by an insatiable thirst for knowledge, based on what you have uncovered so far, you embark on a scholarly pursuit. You delve into dusty tomes, sacred scriptures, and the meticulous notes of excavations past. You pore over the fragmented epics etched into clay tablets and translate the inscriptions on monumental stone, hoping to find more than the mere shadows of these ancient beings.

As you read the Book of Genesis, the records of Flavius Josephus, and the Jewish pseudepigrapha Book of Enoch, you shift your focus towards spiritual matters.

These texts provide some insight into this enduring mystery, although their illumination is somewhat subdued. The stories of their creation are as numerous as they are fanciful.

They survived the Deluge (Flood), some suggest, not by ark or highland refuge, but through celestial favor or otherworldly creative. Could these giants have transformed into demonic spirits following the flood? Is it possible that this is how they managed to endure and survive?

The stories that the giants or the Nephilim could have survived the Great Flood, not through physical means but rather as spiritual entities, is a fascinating concept that has been explored in various religious and mythological texts.

In the Biblical narrative of Genesis, the Nephilim you discover are briefly mentioned before the account of the Flood, and there is no direct mention of their fate afterward. As we have discussed in previous chapters, the Jewish pseudepigrapha Book of Enoch, however, offers a more detailed exposition. According to this text, the Nephilim are the offspring of the "Watchers," a group of fallen angels, and human women.

The Book of Enoch suggests that when the Nephilim were killed, their physical deaths released their spirits onto the earth. These spirits, or "unclean spirits" as they are sometimes called in the Bible, may have persisted after the bodies of the Nephilim perished.

The Book of Enoch goes into further detail, implying that these spirits were not at peace due to their hybrid origin and the manner of their demise. It shows that they roamed the earth as evil entities — possibly the evil spirits or demons that would afflict humanity, thus continuing their existence in a spiritual form.

Flavius Josephus, while not delving into the post-flood existence of the Nephilim, does acknowledge their pre-flood presence and influence, hinting at their potentially enduring impact on human history. He describes them as men of renown of the prehistoric world, which could suggest that their legacy, if not their physical presence, continued after the flood.

Tracing the Nephilim from Scripture to Spirit

As you keep digging you come across the early Christian theological discourse, including the writings of figures such as Tertullian and Augustine, who often associated the Nephilim with the spread of sin and heresy, legitimizing the idea that these beings could have had a spiritual role post-flood as tempters and instigators of mankind's continued fall from grace.

You discover this notion of survival through spiritualization is not unique to the Nephilim narrative. In many religious traditions, the idea that beings could transcend physical destruction and persist as spirits has been a common way to explain the endurance of their influence or presence.

From an archaeological perspective though, such spiritual theories are not easily explored. Instead, the focus is often on tangible evidence: physical remains, cultural artifacts, and historical records that can provide clues about these giants' lives and deaths.

The potential for an entity to survive as a spiritual form is outside the scope of physical archaeology and often enters the realm of theology. Thus, while the idea of the Nephilim transforming into demon spirits postulates a compelling bridge between the physical and spiritual realms, it is a concept best interpreted through the lenses of religious studies.

The Nephilim Giants Did Exist

Narrative:

The existence of giants in the Bible is not a matter of debate, it indeed did happen. Their presence poses intriguing questions about the narrative of the ancient world. The biblical references to giants begin primarily in the book of Genesis and Enoch. The verses in the two books indicate the presence of giants before the flood and after.

The stories that giants could have become evil spirits after the flood and possessed other people to maintain their lineage is an interpretive hypothesis not explicitly found in the Scriptures. Instead, such interpretations arise from linking various biblical passages and apocryphal texts.

As for the notion that Ham's wife might have been a descendant of the Nephilim, this idea is speculative and not directly supported by the biblical text.

It arises from trying to explain the reappearance of the giants post-flood, as mentioned in Numbers 13:33, where the Israelite spies report seeing Nephilim in Canaan: "*And there we saw the giants, the sons of Anak, which come of the giants: and we were in our own sight as grasshoppers, and so we were in their sight.*" Since Noah's son Ham established the land of Canaan, could Ham's wife be a descendant of the giants? Maybe, but it is not important in the grand plan.

The figure of Nimrod, as mentioned in the previous chapter, does come from the lineage of Ham and is described in Genesis 10:8-9 as "a mighty one in the earth" and "a mighty hunter before the LORD." While these descriptions give Nimrod a reputation for exceptional prowess, the Bible does not explicitly describe him as a giant.

Based on ancient writings, there are some things that we are aware of. Personally, however, I find them not very credible or significant. One such thing is that Nimrod, who was also known as Osiris in Egypt, supposedly founded the first world empire at Babel. This empire later came to be known as Babylon (as referenced in Genesis 10:8-12; 11:1-9).

From ancient sources such as the "Epic of Gilgamesh" and records unearthed by archeologists from long-ruined Mesopotamian and Egyptian cities, we can reconstruct subsequent events.

After Nimrod's death (c. 2167 BC), Semiramis promoted the belief that he was a god. She claimed that she saw a full-grown evergreen tree spring out of the roots of a dead tree stump, symbolizing the springing forth of new life for Nimrod. On the anniversary of his birth, she said, Nimrod would visit the evergreen tree and leave gifts under it. His birthday fell on the winter solstice at the end of December.

A few years later, Semiramis bore a son, Horus or Gilgamesh. She declared that she had been visited by the spirit of Nimrod, who left her pregnant with the boy. Horus. I am sharing this only to provide you with another perspective on why some people believe how the giants survived after the flood. However, none of it holds significance in God's grand plan, so we should not give it too much importance.

It is wise not to go down a rabbit trail that has no biblical reference and takes you away from God's truth. With a subject like this, that can easily happen, so be cautious if you choose to delve deeper into it on your own. I share all of the above references with Semiramis in order to illuminate other perspectives.

God Addressed the Wrongdoing Committed by the Nephilim.

The most significant thread running throughout the Bible is not the mysteries of the giants, but rather God's sovereign plan and His dealings with sin. When the Israelites, led by Joshua, enter the land of Canaan, they face the giants in a series of conquests.

This symbolizes God's judgment against sin and His deliverance for His chosen people, as seen in Joshua chapters 10 to 12, culminating with Joshua's declaration in Joshua 21:43-45 that not one of all the good promises the Lord had made to Israel had failed.

The story of David and Goliath in 1 Samuel 17 vividly depicts the eventual defeat of the giants, symbolizing victory over sin and evil. Goliath, described as a giant from Gath, stood as a formidable challenge to the Israelite army, defying the very God they served.

Yet, David, a shepherd boy armed with faith and a sling, overcame the giant, declaring in 1 Samuel 17:45, "*You come to me with a sword and with a spear and with a javelin, but I come to you in the name of the LORD of hosts, the God of the armies of Israel, whom you have defied.*"

This iconic moment underscores the Bible's overarching message that God's power and purposes are not hindered by physical might or the seeming impossibilities of human circumstances.

The battles against the giants throughout the Promised Land can also be seen as part of the divine purification process, preparing a holy land for a holy people.

This theme is consistent with statements found in Deuteronomy 9:1-5, where it is clear that the conquest is an act of divine justice delivered by God and not a result of Israel's righteousness.

The giants' occupation of the land portrays a physical barrier to the Israelites' inheritance but more importantly, signifies the spiritual opposition against the establishment of a covenantal nation under God.

Furthermore, the consequences of sin and the hope of redemption encapsulated in these stories foreshadow the redemptive work of Jesus Christ. The sin of the Watchers in Genesis 6, leading to the Nephilim and subsequent corruption, demanded divine intervention. Similarly, the sin of humanity necessitated a Savior.

The New Testament Vision of the Messiah's Arrival

The New Testament then unfolds this plan, as evidenced by Galatians 4:4-5, which says, "*But when the fullness of time had come, God sent forth his Son, born of woman, born under the law, to redeem those who were under the law, so that we might receive adoption as sons.*"

This redemptive motif is echoed in the virgin birth, signifying a pure and holy inception for the Messiah, distinct from the tainted origins of the Nephilim. We know this from Luke 1:35: *"And the angel answered her, 'The Holy Spirit will come upon you, and the power of the Most High will overshadow you; therefore the child to be born will be called holy —the Son of 'God.'* The Nephilim were born in sin, but Jesus was born holy.

In the same way, as the coming of Joshua to the Promised Land marked a new beginning for Israel, so too did the arrival of Jesus signify a new covenant and ultimate victory over sin and death.

Where the law and human effort fell short, His sinless life, atoning death, and resurrection accomplished what was impossible for humanity. As Romans 5:17 explains, "*For if, because of one man's trespass, death reigned through that one man, much more will those who receive the abundance of grace."* The sin of the watchers was a very big sin and it took Jesus to finally reverse the curse of this Grand Rebellion in His virgin birth.

This divine intervention rendered the transgressions of the Watchers null through a singular, sanctified act: the conception of Jesus. In an immaculate reversal of the Watchers' corruption, God chose Mary—a vessel of purity—to bring forth His Son.

Unlike the Nephilim's inception in rebellion, Jesus's birth was steeped in holiness, marking a critical step in overcoming humanity's fall. His entrance into the world laid the groundwork; His resurrection sealed the overthrow of the ancient curse for all time, rectifying the divine-human relationship irreversibly. This act concludes the 2nd Grand Rebellion. In the next chapter, we will discuss the third and final rebellion in the Tower of Babel Sin.

Chapter 11

Tower of Babel Sin

Opening Scene:

As you embark on the journey of this chapter, imagine yourself abruptly arriving in a realm reshaped by cataclysmic events. The echoes of a great flood linger in the air, whispers of a tragedy that swept away entire generations, sparing only a select few. You find yourself among the voices of the aftermath, recounting tales of survival and loss.

In the wake of this upheaval, a luminescent rainbow stretches across the skies, arresting your gaze with its dazzling spectrum. Time seems to stand still as you bask for hours in its radiant symphony of colors—each hue a silent promise of renewal and continuity.

Venturing deeper into this reborn landscape, the sight of imposing mountains strikes you—majestic sentinels rising high above the plains you've known. The invigorating mountain air fills your lungs, reminiscent of the clear, rejuvenating mornings among high altitudes. With each breath, hope swells in your chest, for this reborn expanse offers not just the prospect of recovery but the perceivable promise of a new dawn.

Overwhelmed by the stirring tides of emotion, your heart holds tight to the montage of experiences that have defined your journey. It commenced in a realm that could only be likened to paradise, where encounters with divine entities struck you with a profound mixture of reverence and trepidation. There, in the celestial stillness, you encountered an awe that rendered you speechless.

Then came the discovery of a garden, graceful in its allure, a place so entrancing that language seems an inadequate vessel to convey its splendor. In that sacred haven, tranquil peace overwhelmed you, and you were touched by a depth of love beyond any you had known. Could this be the Garden of Eden once more? Has God's grand plan been fulfilled?

Witnessing the Fall of a Divine Order

Then you find yourself outside of this peaceful garden experience. Here you see a crumbling civilization awash with chaos, where sin's shadow reached far and wide. Observing the heavens breach, as angelic figures descended to mingle with humankind, you bore witness to the ingression of giants and rampant divine defiance.

The oppressive darkness of this decaying world evoked memories of worlds you had seen in the past. This weighed heavily upon you, leaving your spirit burdened with despair and void of hope. You thought that this chaos was behind you, but you realized that there is still one more grand rebellion that God has to deal with.

Shadows of Babel: Nimrod, the Ziggurat, and Echoes of the Giants

Now, as you progress through the years, you stumble upon a bustling city in this new world, where people gather. Among them, you spot a man named Nimrod, whom you realize is descended from Ham, Noah's son. He leads the people in constructing a triangular ziggurat-like structure, yet you sense their worship is not aligned with God's intentions.

This brings up feelings similar to what you experienced in the previous world of rebellion against God. Deep within, you sense that something significant must happen to correct this course, a feeling intertwined with your very being. Notably, you observe that Nimrod stands taller than others, almost resembling a giant. Curiosity arises as you remember the possibility of giants surviving the flood.

Suddenly, a remarkable sighting on Earth mirrors an occurrence you once witnessed in heaven. The council of God is observed walking among the people, exchanging thoughts amongst themselves. The details of their conversation elude you, yet their actions result in a sudden change.

A multitude of different languages emerge, causing people to seek out others who speak their language. Tribes begin to form, and individuals depart from the city, dispersing to various parts of the world.

Your intrigue grew, and a thirst for further knowledge consumed you. Yet, frustratingly, the opportunity to uncover what lay ahead was withheld from you.

You listen intently as a voice reveals the existence of another significant sin, one that holds great relevance to the importance of Jesus. The voice started to explain to you that what you have just witnessed is the sin described in Genesis 11:1-9, commonly known as the story of the Tower of Babel.

Within this account, it is revealed that the entire world shared a common language and spoke the same words. In this time, Noah's great-grandson, Nimrod, established a region called Ancient Mesopotamia in the land of Shinar.

You were told that the sin doesn't emerge until verse 4, where a collective desire is voiced: "*Come, let us build ourselves a city and a tower with its top in the heavens, and let us make a name for ourselves, lest we be dispersed over the face of the whole earth.*" This event takes place after the devastating flood, displaying mankind's susceptibility to succumb to Satan's temptation to idolize themselves.

Narrative:

Remember from the beginning that God created man to worship Him and to have fellowship with Him; He never created man to elevate oneself above God. God's promise by sending the rainbow was to never destroy the earth again by flood, so His only choice here was to remove His presence from all of mankind and establish a kingdom on earth unto Himself, Israel.

God Establishes a Nation Through Abraham

Right after the Tower of Babel incident, God called Abraham in Genesis 12:2 to be set apart as His chosen people to bring about God's divine plan that through his seed, God's nation will be established here on earth.

So, what happens to the nations that God did not choose? Let's explore further into the fall of these nations but first let's unpack more what you saw when the divine council came to the earth.

In Genesis 11:5, Yahweh came down with His divine council to earth to personally witness what was happening with the people of Mesopotamia. This demonstrates that God, also known as Yahweh or Jesus in human form, made several appearances on earth before the coming of Jesus the Messiah.

Many people are unaware of these instances. During this visit, God and His council determined that it was not ideal for humankind to possess a single language.

In verse 7, it states, "*Come, let us go down and there confuse their language, so that they may not understand one another's speech.*" It is important to note the use of the word "us" in this context. This signifies that God is one entity, as stated in Deuteronomy 6:4, rather than three separate entities as some may have previously associated with the notion of the Trinity.

The "us" here refers to His council, with whom He involves with His decision-making. Similarly, our own humankind council of prayer and meditation holds great importance.

God and humankind have always been interconnected, working together by prayer. Prayer plays a crucial role in our relationship with God, as He listens to our hearts and communicates His will to us.

His divine creation carries out His plan for us, and together we exist in harmony. This text teaches us the importance of communication with others and with God.

Everything always goes through Him, His creation either accepts Him as God or rebels against Him. God desires fellowship and a relationship with humankind, just as He does with His divine council.

Divine Estrangement and the Nations

Now let's turn our attention to the other nations that were formed after the fall of Babel. This is very important to understand because this has to do with the reverse of order that Jesus came to make right.

After the fall of Babel God completely turned his back on mankind and began His divine plan of establishing Israel as His chosen nation. The world was now fully turned over to Satan and the sons of God now controlled the nations.

We know this because of what we read in Deuteronomy 32:8-9 *"When the Most High Yahweh gave to the nations their inheritance when he divided mankind (Babel), he fixed the borders of the peoples according to the number of the sons of God (Elohim Watchers). But the Lord's portion is his people, Jacob (Aka Israel) His allotted heritage."*

In Matthew 4:1-11, we witness the moment when Satan tempts Jesus. In verse 8, Satan says, *"I will give you all the kingdoms of the world,"* and in verse 9, he adds, *"All these I will give you if you fall down and worship me."* This raises the question: why would Satan make such an offer?

The answer lies in the fact that God had turned His back on the nations and could not associate Himself with sin. These verses highlight that the world, at that time, was under the dominion of Satan. However, everything changed when Jesus died and rose again. His sacrifice opened the door for the world to have fellowship with God, but only if they aligned themselves with God's chosen nation.

Therefore, the temptations faced by Jesus were not just personal trials but symbolic of the struggle for the ownership of the world. It is through Jesus' victory over Satan that we have the opportunity to restore our relationship with God, allowing us to experience the fellowship that was once lost.

The final overturning of the third rebellion took place in Acts 2 during the momentous event of Pentecost, following Jesus' resurrection. In Genesis 10, often referred to as the "table of Nations," we find a comprehensive list of the known nations at that time.

Depending on the text, the number of nations is either 70 in the Masoretic text (Hebrew) or 72 in the Septuagint (Greek). This number is significant as it takes us back to the Babel incident. Dr. Michael Heiser refers to this number as "cosmic geography," emphasizing the battle for land and territory.

Of all the nations, Israel stands as the portion belonging to Yahweh Himself. The other nations, on the other hand, are assigned to lesser Elohim, delegated to the authority of the sons of God.

This allocation of nations to various deities is a consequence of the punishment following the Babel incident. So, why did God do this? By disinheriting and assigning them to other gods, He set the stage for His ultimate purpose. He knew all along that His resurrection was going to reverse this rebellion once and for all.

Promptly after punishing the nations and their placement under other gods, God calls Abraham. Through Abraham and his descendants, He declares that all the nations of the earth will be blessed and His once again.

But how?

Thus, the events in Acts 2, with the outpouring of the Holy Spirit at Pentecost, signify the culmination of that reversal. The nations, once divided, are now being reached and blessed through the message of salvation in Jesus Christ. The battle for cosmic geography has shifted, and God's redemptive plan encompasses the entire earth, fulfilling His promise to Abraham and bringing blessings to all nations.

Unveiling the Mystery of the Scroll in Revelation 5

In the Book of Revelation, Chapter 5, we find ourselves immersed in a vivid, celestial picture with John as our guide. Within this divine panorama, Jesus is portrayed at the center of the heavenly throne room, surrounded by God and the assembly of elders. A pivotal moment arises with the inquiry, "Who is worthy to open the scroll?"

This scroll is extremely important, symbolizing the title deed to the Earth. Now that we understand that after the Tower of Babel, God rejected man with Satan and other gods as its ruler. In Revelation 5, everything now becomes clearer regarding what the scroll represents and why. Let's turn to the scriptures and read this passage to understand the context of this scene fully.

> *"Then I saw in the right hand of him who was seated on the throne a scroll written within and on the back, sealed with seven seals. And I saw a mighty angel proclaiming with a loud voice, "Who is worthy to open the scroll and break its seals?" And no one in heaven or on earth or under the earth was able to open the scroll or to look into it, and I began to weep loudly because no one was found worthy to open the scroll or to look into it. And one of the elders said to me, "Weep no more; behold, the Lion of the tribe of Judah, the Root of David, has conquered, so that he can open the scroll and its seven seals."* (Revelations 5:1-5)

With Jesus' resurrection, he now has the rightful claim to Earth, all things are restored to their intended glory. This chapter is a powerful testament to His redemptive work. However, to appreciate the magnitude of this restoration, we must explore the events of Pentecost further.

Unveiling the Deeper Connection in Acts

The New Testament holds significant relevance to this subject, particularly in the book of Acts, specifically during the time of Pentecost. While many of us are familiar with this story, there are deeper aspects that we may not fully grasp. In Acts 2, on the day of Pentecost, the believers were gathered in one place when suddenly, there came a sound like a rushing wind, filling the entire house. Divided tongues, resembling fire, appeared among them.

Here, I want to draw attention to the word "divided." In the Greek translation of the Old Testament, the word for "divided" appears in Deuteronomy 32:8, where it speaks of the Most High dividing up the nations. Acts 2 strategically uses this vocabulary from Deuteronomy 32, linking it to the events at Pentecost. But why would Luke do this? Let's look deeper.

Continuing in Acts 2:5, we discover that devout Jews from various nations under heaven were dwelling in Jerusalem at the time. As the sound spread, a multitude gathered, bewildered by the extraordinary occurrences. Each person heard the disciples speaking in their own language. Again, I want to highlight the word "bewildered," which, in Greek, is connected to Genesis 11, the incident of the Tower of Babel when the nations were divided.

Luke, through these intentional connections, seeks to make his readers reflect on the significance of the Pentecost event in relation to the dividing of nations in Genesis 11 and Deuteronomy 32. By mentally revisiting this event, readers can understand that it serves as the backdrop and framework for what unfolds in Acts 2.

As we read further into Acts 2, we witness the outpouring of the Holy Spirit upon the followers of Jesus, empowering them to speak in various languages. It is crucial to note that present at Pentecost were Jews from nations all over the known world. These Jews were dwelling in different nations due to historical events such as the exile and the displacement of people.

Through the divine timing of Pentecost, many of them had returned to Jerusalem after the resurrection of Jesus. They would come to hear Peter's message and witness the wonders of Acts 2, including the rushing wind and the ability to communicate the gospel in different languages. This infiltration, orchestrated by God, involves the inclusion of the nations in His grand plan of salvation.

Acts 2 represents God's ultimate act of complete redemption for mankind. Through His resurrection and the indwelling of the Holy Spirit, God has reestablished divine order in the world, granting humanity restored access to His throne room.

Empowered by faith, we hold sway over every dominion and power that stakes a claim on this earth. In the name of Jesus, victory is ours, and we are called to be a beacon of hope in a realm still under the influence of Satan.

Armed with the keys to spiritual liberation, it is our divine mandate to disseminate these truths across humanity. The intricacies of this empowerment will be expounded upon in future chapters.

But as we conclude this section, we acknowledge that Jesus has rectified the Three Grand Rebellions chronicled in Scripture. This momentous transformation beckons us to ponder: What is next for my life? In the chapters ahead, we will explore the profound role of Jesus as the Redeemer and unravel the expectations placed upon humanity in our contemporary era.

Before we unpack the responsibilities and implications that follow in the wake of redemption, let us first reflect upon the prophecies Jesus fulfilled, bringing this divine restoration into reality.

The odds of these ancient predictions coming to pass may seem extraordinarily improbable, verging on the impossible. Yet, for those who walk in the footsteps of Christ, these fulfilled prophecies are not merely historical milestones; they are cornerstones that strengthen and affirm the foundation of our faith in Jesus.

Chapter 12

Prophecy and Fulfillment

Opening Scene:

As with other chapters, envision yourself as the lead actor in a sci-fi cinematic movie, where the opening scene has you, stepping into a room that transcends ordinary reality.

Before you stretches a vast wall adorned with what resemble computer screens, these are conduits to something far beyond mere technology. In this chamber of wonders, the veil of time is lifted, granting you a panoramic view of the past, present, and future—scenes and stories unfold as if woven from the very fabric of existence.

As you attempt to comprehend everything you are witnessing, you hear Psalms 147:5 being softly spoken within your soul: *"Our Lord is truly great and immensely powerful; his understanding knows no bounds"*.

Trying to grapple with the enormity of this spectacle, one thing becomes abundantly clear: you stand at the nexus of two worlds. There's the spiritual realm, indescribable and resplendent, governed by divine wisdom; and its counterpart, the physical world, where flesh navigates a reality of limited insight, bound by the unfolding of cosmic cause and effect.

In this hallowed place, a profound synthesis occurs: the divine spirit imparts sacred knowledge to the flesh, guiding humanity towards a more prosperous and fulfilling existence that best glorifies God.

You read Hebrews 4:13 *"Nothing in all creation is hidden from God's sight. Everything is uncovered and laid bare before the eyes of him to whom we must give account"*.

With this knowledge, you realize, that from your advantage point, you can reach out to individuals across space and time. Your voice is carried on celestial wings, in the words of those who heed the divine whispers, or even through orchestrated events that gently nudge souls toward their greater good.

You see flashed up on the screen Acts 15:18 *"Known unto God are all his works from the beginning of the world"*.

That leads you to cry out Psalms 139:1-4 *"You have searched me, Lord, and you know me. You know when I sit and when I rise; you perceive my thoughts from afar. You discern my going out and my lying down; you are familiar with all my ways. Before a word is on my tongue you, Lord, know it completely."*

Witnessing the Divine Choreography of Destiny

As your gaze humbly pierces into the unknown, foretelling the destinies of people and the grand narrative of all things, there exists a sense of cosmic choreography—each movement deliberate, every scene purposeful. You witness lives aligned with this celestial cadence flourish in harmony with the divine design, while those that spurn it seem to spiral into death that leads to hell for all eternity.

Bible verses automatically appear to assist you in understanding what you're seeing. Like Galatians 6:7-10 *"Do not be deceived: God cannot be mocked. A man reaps what he sows. The one who sows to please his sinful nature, from that nature will reap destruction; the one who sows to please the Spirit, from the Spirit will reap eternal life."*

Yet, amidst the apparent disarray of the fleshly plane, your sanctuary is an enclave of serenity. Herein lies the outline of tranquility, a peace indescribable that words falter to encapsulate. Amidst the widescreen spectacle of life's boundless story, your soul bathes in the resounding calm—a testament to the sublime order governing the dance of the cosmos.

As you beheld the unfolding panorama, transcending time and space, a profound sense of love covers you—a love so deep and boundless that it transcended all your prior experiences and understanding. The Bible verse John 3:16 *"For God so love the world"*, took on a new significance, you finally grasped the enormity of this love. This wasn't simply an emotion; it was a force, a living current that pulsed through history with intentional grace.

You were escorted on a journey through the archives of humankind, witnessing the immutable thread of divine affection carefully woven into the tapestry of human existence. The experience transported you to the time of Jesus, where you saw the depth of His love for humanity—a constant and unwavering presence throughout the ages.

Your mind, abuzz with questions, found solace in the immediacy of answers, each inquiry met with swift understanding. The Divine, God Himself, revealed the intricacy of His master plan—a design that has, since the dawn of time, held His creation in tender regard.

Visions of prophets and seers bestowed upon humanity cascaded before you, divine prophecies foretelling the coming Messiah. Through human eyes, the fulfillment of such promises seemed an impossibility, a narrative fraught with implausible divine intervention.

But, standing in this room, where the horizon of all potential stretched into eternity, you came to an epiphany: within the realm of God, no notion is beyond reach, no miracle beyond manifesting. Here, in the presence of the Almighty, you realize the true essence of faith—for with God, nothing is impossible.

Jesus Fulfills over 300 Prophecies

Narrative:

Now back on earth humans know that within the New Testament narrative, the figure of Jesus emerges as the fulfillment of an array of ancient prophecies foretold in the Old Testament scriptures.

While the exact tally of these prophecies is a matter of scholarly debate, with interpretations varying across the theological spectrum, Christian theologians and apologists often reference a figure exceeding 300 prophetic connections made manifest through Jesus's life, ministry, death, and resurrection.

This substantial number is not uniformly accepted, as the criteria to classify a prophecy as directly, thematically, or typologically fulfilled by Jesus can differ significantly among scholars. Some see Jesus's actions and words as direct fulfillments of specific verses, while others find a broader, more allegorical connection in the types and shadows prefiguring Christ within the Old Testament.

The figure of over 300 prophecies is derived from the cumulative efforts of numerous Christian authors and researchers who, over the years, have meticulously collated verses from the Hebrew Bible, interpreting these as clear messianic indicators pointing unequivocally toward Jesus as the awaited Messiah.

It should be acknowledged that interpretations outside of Christian tradition often contrast sharply with these assertions. Jewish scholars, those of other faiths, and secular historians typically apply a different hermeneutic approach to the Hebrew Scriptures, thereby not recognizing the same passages as messianic promises, let alone fulfilling them in the person of Jesus.

The discourse surrounding messianic prophecies is, therefore, deeply enriched by a variety of religious and intellectual perspectives, each bringing a unique lens through which the ancient texts are understood and the narrative of fulfillment is woven.

17 Prophecies Fulfilled with Little Doubt

Despite the complexities and nuances of biblical prophecy, there are several well-known prophetic passages from the Old Testament that we can safely say Jesus unmistakably fulfilled. Or at the very least, you can decide for yourself, but for me, these 17 seem quite apparent.

1. **Virgin Birth:** Isaiah 7:14 prophesies a virgin birth, a prophecy Christians believe reaches its fulfillment with the birth of Jesus to Mary as recorded in Matthew 1:22-23.

2. **Birthplace in Bethlehem:** The prophet Micah, in 5:2, pinpoints Bethlehem as the Messiah's birthplace. This detail aligns seamlessly with the narrative of Jesus's birth described in Matthew 2:4-6.

3. **The lineage of David:** Scriptural passages such as 2 Samuel 7:12-16 assert that the Messiah would descend from King David's lineage, a claim substantiated by the genealogies presented in Matthew 1 and Luke 3 that trace Jesus's heritage back to David.

4. **A Prophet Like Moses:** In Deuteronomy 18:15, Moses tells of a prophet to come who would resemble him, which Acts 3:20-22 confirms as being Jesus.

5. **Entrance into Jerusalem:** The prophet Zechariah foretells in 9:9 of a king arriving in Jerusalem on a donkey, an event echoed in the New Testament when Jesus enters the city as mentioned in Matthew 21:4-5.

6. **Betrayal for Silver:** In Zechariah 11:12-13, there is the mention of thirty pieces of silver as the price of betrayal—later seen fulfilled in the New Testament account of Judas's actions in Matthew 26:14-15.

7. **Crucifixion Imagery:** The imagery found in Psalm 22:16 of pierced hands and feet is considered to prefigure the crucifixion, which is recounted in John 19:34-37.

8. **Silent Before Accusers:** Isaiah 53:7 speaks of a messianic figure who would remain silent in the face of accusations, a portrayal fitting the account of Jesus's trial in Matthew 27:12-14.

9. **Resurrection:** Passages like Psalm 16:10 and Isaiah 53:10-11 are interpreted as hints of the Messiah's resurrection, an event which the New Testament narrates, notably in Luke 24:6-7.

10. **The Messianic Miracles:** Isaiah 35:5-6 depicts a time when the eyes of the blind will be opened and the ears of the deaf unstopped. This is seen as fulfilled in the healing miracles of Jesus, such as in Matthew

11:5, where it is reported that, "the blind receive sight, the lame walk, those who have leprosy are cured, the deaf hear, the dead are raised, and the good news is preached to the poor.

11. **Rejected by His Own People:** Psalm 69:8 and Isaiah 53:3 speak of the Messiah being rejected by his own people. This is reflected in the New Testament, where Jesus is rejected by the Jewish leaders and by the people, as in John 1:11 where it says, *"He came to that which was his own, but his own did not receive him."*

12. **Taking Our Infirmities:** Isaiah 53:4-5 is seen as a prediction of Christ's atoning sacrifice, bearing our sicknesses and carrying our sorrows. This is cited in Matthew 8:16-17, where Jesus heals the sick, fulfilling what was spoken through the prophet Isaiah.

13. **The Triumphal Entry:** Zechariah 9:9 predicts the coming of Zion's King, riding on a donkey; this is seen as a direct reference to Jesus' triumphal entry into Jerusalem, as narrated in Luke 19:35-38.

14. **Died With Transgressors:** Isaiah 53:12 foretells the suffering servant would be *"numbered with the transgressors,"* which Christians believe was fulfilled when Jesus was crucified between two thieves, as depicted in Mark 15:27-28.

15. **No Bones Broken:** Psalm 34:20 states, *"He protects all his bones, not one of them will be broken,"* which is seen to correspond with the fact that Jesus' legs were

not broken during the crucifixion, as was the custom; this is fulfilled according to John 19:33-36.

16. **The Casting of Lots for His Garments:** Psalm 22:18 anticipates that people would cast lots for the Messiah's clothes. This event occurs during Jesus' crucifixion, as detailed in Matthew 27:35.

17. **His Side Pierced:** Zechariah 12:10 includes a prophecy that *"They will look on me, the one they have pierced, and they will mourn for him as one mourns for an only child, and grieve bitterly for him as one grieves for a firstborn son."* Detailed in John 19:34

The Probability of Jesus Fulfilling Prophecies.

The remarkable odds of a single individual fulfilling an extensive slate of detailed prophecies have long captured the intellectual curiosity of Christian apologists. They utilize this astounding improbability to bolster the case for Jesus' authentic messianic identity.

Peter Stoner's "Science Speaks" stands out among discussions, leveraging the laws of probability to illuminate the unlikelihood of one person realizing even a handful of specific biblical prophecies.

Stoner's statistical analysis focused on EIGHT distinct prophecies, leading to the conclusion that the odds of one individual fulfilling all of them were 1 in 10^{17}, or one in one hundred quadrillions. The sheer magnitude of this statistic is best apprehended through Stoner's vivid analogy:

Envision blanketing the entire state of Texas with 10^{17} silver dollars, until they lay two feet thick. Imagine marking just one of these coins and stirring it into the expansive sea of silver. A person, blindfolded, is then given the liberty to wander at will but must ultimately select a single coin.

The probability that the first coin they pick would be the marked one is similar to the chance of eight prophecies coming to fruition in one person, assuming the prophets authored their writings based on their own wisdom.

Pushing the envelope of probability even further, Stoner applied his calculations to 48 prophecies, arriving at a staggering probability of 1 in 10^{157}—an abstract number that skirts the edges of human comprehension.

Christian apologists point to these astronomical figures to argue that mere chance could not account for the prophetic fulfillment evident in the life of Jesus. They contend that such precise alignment between prophecy and historical occurrence must point to a narrative intricately woven by divine design.

Exploring the Probability of Fulfillment Deeper

From my perspective, Jesus has clearly fulfilled the 17 prophecies that I have listed. Interestingly enough, experts have also explored the scenario of Jesus fulfilling a set of 16 prophecies and beyond, shedding light on the probabilities involved in such an occurrence. Here's what they discovered in their study.

In order for 16 Prophecies to be fulfilled, we must consider the probability of an individual uniquely fulfilling a single prophecy at odds of 1 in 10. Now, extend that to the fulfillment of 16 distinct prophecies.

The compounded likelihood plummets to a staggering 1 in 10^16, a number representing ten multiplied by itself 16 times. This scenario is reminiscent of searching for a uniquely marked grain of sand within a colossal collection, enough to fill a million average living room spaces.

What if Jesus fulfilled 300 Prophecies, what would the probability be then? Venturing into the prospects of one individual meeting the criteria of over 300 prophecies, we come to a figure that eludes the grasp of conventional probability theory and eclipses our capacity for visualization.

No earthly or cosmic comparison seems adequate to truly convey the magnitude of such odds, for they span beyond our ordinary scales of measurement or comprehension, underscoring a complexity that suggests more than mere chance or coincidence.

To further underscore the analytical approach toward understanding the probability of prophecy fulfillment, consider the illustrative work done by a professor from Westmont College. The focal point of this investigation is the science of probability, which seeks to ascertain the likelihood of a specific event taking place.

This particular professor, collaborating with approximately 600 university students across twelve different classes, embarked on a rigorous examination of the major prophecies concerning the Messiah.

The students engaged in deep discussions, meticulously considering each prophecy, and assessing any potential for human collaboration in achieving fulfillment. Aiming for a conservative consensus, they deliberated until even the skeptics among them could agree on the plausibility of the figures proposed.

Yet, taking a step further towards caution, the professor refined these numbers, making them even more conservative, and openly challenged skeptics and scientists alike to conduct their own estimations to test the fairness of his conclusions.

To validate the integrity of this scholarly endeavor, the professor's calculations were presented to a committee from the American Scientific Affiliation. After meticulous review, this committee confirmed the reliability and accuracy of his work concerning the scientific data.

One of the striking examples shared was based on the prophecy of Micah 5:2, which foretells the birthplace of the Messiah as Bethlehem. The professor and his students calculated the average population of Bethlehem from Micah's time until today and compared it to the world population over the same period.

Their determination? The probability of any one person being born in Bethlehem was calculated to be one in 300,000 — showcasing the incredibly specific nature of such prophecies and the extraordinary likelihood of their concurrent fulfillment in a single individual.

As the professor concludes, "Any man who rejects Christ as the Son of God is rejecting a fact, proved perhaps more absolutely than any other fact in the world."

Probability in Familiar Terms

Probability, often expressed in the familiar term "odds," is a mathematical concept that evaluates the likelihood of a particular event coming to pass. To put the concept of probability into perspective and to better contextualize our discussion, let's delve into some intriguing examples of "odds" that shed light on just how improbable certain events are.

Having Twins= 1 in 250

Being Bitten by a shark= 1 in 12,000

Being struck by lightning in a year = 7 x 105 or 1 in 700,000

Being killed by lightning in a year = 2 x 106 or 1 in 2,000,000

Becoming president = 1 x 107 or 1 in 10,000,000

A meteorite landing on your house = 1.8 x 1014 or 1 in 180,000,000,000,000

You will eventually die = 1 in 1

The probabilities tied to uncommon occurrences in our daily lives—like surviving a lightning strike, ascending to the presidency, or encountering a meteorite on one's property

—offer a glimpse into the realm of the statistically improbable. When we shift our focus to the prophetic fulfillments attributed to Jesus, we are confronted with a scale of improbability that dwarfs these already staggering events.

The odds of any single individual fulfilling a vast array of detailed and interwoven prophecies, as Jesus has done, stretch beyond the boundaries of our typical understanding of chance.

Unlike the random occurrences that might affect any person by mere happenstance, the prophecies said to be realized in Jesus are intricately specific, encompassing an array of times, places, and conditions that intertwine with historical narratives.

When examining the likelihood of Jesus meeting the criteria of just a handful of these predictions, let alone over 300, we step into an arena where the traditional concepts of probability strain under the weight of such astronomical odds.

The realization dawns that the convergence of these prophecies in a single life seems to surpass mere coincidence—it suggests a grand design or higher purpose beyond ordinary comprehension.

In the domain of faith and belief, the question of probability becomes not just a mathematical wonder but a reflection on the nature of divine purpose and intervention. Believers find that the fulfillment of such intricate prophecies in the person of Jesus affirms their faith in a providential narrative, one where every thread is intentionally woven, and what is statistically improbable becomes spiritually profound.

The probabilities of Jesus fulfilling Bible Prophecy Strengthens our Faith.

The conviction that Jesus fulfilled biblical prophecies is a cornerstone of the Christian faith, serving as a profound testament to the continuity and divine inspiration of Scripture. This belief not only underscores the sovereignty and foreknowledge of God but also deeply enriches our understanding and interpretation of the Bible.

By recognizing the meshing of prophecy and fulfillment, we gain a multi-dimensional view of our faith, where the realms of history, spirituality, and divine revelation converge, offering a cohesive narrative that guides and sustains believers through our journey of life.

In the end, the significance of Jesus's fulfillment of prophecy is multifaceted. For believers, it forms a key part of the fabric of Christian apologetics and doctrine, reinforcing the claim that Jesus is the unique and preordained savior of the world.

Having looked into the extraordinary probability of Jesus fulfilling biblical prophecy, we now transition to the next chapter: understanding Jesus as the great Redeemer.

Belief in Jesus as God and the fulfillment of prophecy is a foundational aspect of the Christian faith, but grasping the profound impact of His redemptive work is pivotal to appreciating how it transforms our lives and enlightens our understanding of purpose.

It is one matter to recognize His divinity and prophetic role; it is entirely another to comprehend the depth of His influence on our personal existence and the discovery of our true calling.

Chapter 13

Jesus the Redeemer

Opening Scene:

As we embark on this chapter, picture yourself walking along a road, reminiscent of the enchanting paths we've seen in movies like "The Wizard of Oz." Although the color and composition of this road is unlike anything we have ever encountered, we know that we are not in heaven but here on earth.

Curiously, it feels as though we have somehow undergone a transformation, allowing us to experience glimpses of the Kingdom of God while still journeying in this earthly realm. This road, it becomes clear, ultimately leads to the eternal city.

Amidst our journey, we come across other roads, broader and seemingly more inviting, promising excitement and adventure. Signposts along these alternative paths beckon us to explore them. Yet, deep within us, the Holy Spirit whispers a different message. It tells us that these roads do not lead to the eternal city, reminding us of the hardships and pain that Jesus has already redeemed and saved us from.

The Holy Spirit encourages us to remain steadfast, to continue walking the straight and narrow road, resisting the allure of those tempting alternatives. He reminds us that by staying close to Jesus through prayer, study of His word, and fellowship, we can find the strength to overcome these temptations.

In this journey, we are not alone. We are accompanied by numerous friends who are also walking alongside us. By engaging in fellowship with them, we find support, encouragement, and accountability. Together, we are able to steer clear of the seductions presented by those alluring paths. Walking in unity, we stay on course, keeping our eyes fixed on Jesus who awaits us in the eternal city.

Tracing God's Persistent Pursuit of Fellowship

In this manner, as we traverse the unfamiliar yet captivating road, guided by the Holy Spirit and supported by fellow believers, we navigate the challenges and overcome the enticements that could potentially divert us from our ultimate destination.

A heavenly voice reveals to you that there is a consistent and unbroken single thread – that exists throughout the pages of the Bible. That thread represents Jesus and God's unconditional love for humanity and His strong desire to have a close relationship with us. Even after mankind's departure from the garden, because of sin, God has always provided a pathway (Road) for us to return to Him.

Narrative:

He relentlessly pursues us, demonstrating profound care and infinite patience. God's ultimate goal has always been to have fellowship with us, and He has meticulously planned a way to redeem us. It is important to note that God has never abandoned us; rather, it is we who have repeatedly turned away from Him.

The road we were on was the road to salvation and it has always existed through faith. Those who believed in God and actively sought Him were always welcomed onto His sacred path. Even more, God made this road to salvation even more accessible to all of humanity through the sacrifice of His Son. Now the entire world no longer needs to remain trapped and subjugated under Satan's influence.

Easter the Fulfillment of God's Grand Plan

Easter is a celebration no other deity can rival, for it represents a unique narrative within the tapestry of faiths. While many religions since their inception promote the idea that salvation or Nirvana must be earned through a showcase of good deeds, the message of Easter tells a different story.

It is a story of the God of the Bible, Yahweh, whose unfaltering commitment to humanity is unmatched. This God exhibits a depth of patience, grace, and mercy beyond our wildest imaginings.

Unlike the teachings of many religions, where followers must seek out their god, Yahweh defies this notion by seeking out His creation. His pursuit is not a mere search; it is a passionate quest for a deep, intimate fellowship with us. It is this unyielding desire that we honor at Easter, reflecting on a God whose love is proactive, never giving up on humanity, and offering a relationship that comes not from our striving, but through His gracious invitation.

Divine Intertwined with Humanity

The miraculous conception of Jesus, as told in Matthew 1:18, illuminates God's sanctified approach to intertwining the Divine with humanity. This verse signifies God's solution—His pure and holy means to enter the human story—contrasting sharply with the grave sin committed by the Watchers, who in Gen 6 are described as having physical relations with humans. The immaculate conception stands as an antithesis to that sin, paving the way for a profound understanding of salvation.

Jesus epitomized a flawless life, setting forth an example for us to emulate. In John 20:22, Jesus imparts the Holy Spirit upon us, equipping us to transcend the boundaries of our human limitations.

Empowered by the Spirit, we are offered the remarkable prospect of achieving feats even greater than those Jesus accomplished during His time on earth, as per His own prophetic words in John 14:12. The path to salvation is, thus, laid bare before us—a path of purity, reflection, and empowered action.

The narrative of redemption is woven intricately through-out Scripture, with God's intention to restore harmony to His creation. This grand plan is hinted at across the tapestry of the Old Testament, where the prophets spoke in veiled terms of what was to come—whispers of the "mysteries of God," as Paul the Apostle would later refer to them in texts like Ephesians 3:3-6.

In the wake of Jesus' resurrection, the disciples experienced an epiphany; the teachings of their Master suddenly came together, revealing the truth that had been obscured from their eyes.

This revelation was orchestrated carefully by Jesus, Himself, who maintained the element of surprise against His adver-sary, Satan. Had the enemy fathomed the depth of God's plan, he surely would have thwarted the crucifixion, which ironically, became the fulcrum of salvation.

Throughout the Old Testament, Jesus made pre-incarnate appearances, familiar to Satan—but these instances were merely the prelude to His ultimate strategy: to reclaim the world for His Kingdom, as is prefigured in books like Daniel 7:13-14.

To enact this divine plan, Jesus, the Son of God, entered our world embodying the life God had always envisioned for hu-mankind. He lived untainted by sin, a pristine life, thereby offering a covering for the transgression Adam engaged within the Garden of Eden, as chronicled in Genesis 3.

God's nature is holy, setting the standard for communion with Him. Mankind must mirror this holiness to be in His presence, an axiom affirmed in Hebrews 12:14. Jesus's life and sacrifice provided the means for us to approach God—in essence, through Christ's holiness, we are granted access to the very throne room of the Most High.

Jesus' blood and resurrection reestablished oneness with the Father so that all man can now come into God's presence. Sin brought us death but Jesus' resurrection brought us eternal life, His resurrection reversed the curse. Mankind still has to make a choice to believe in Jesus and willingly surrender their control over to the Father.

The difference being that in Jesus's name, we are no longer separated from the Father or denied salvation because of our sin. Death (aka Satan) is defeated and victory over all sin is now attainable for us.

In this world mankind has an evil heart and sin is prominent with man. With Jesus' death and resurrection, we are now given the Holy Spirit to live inside of us to help us learn all things, John 14:26, so that we can overcome our sin.

Romans 8:12-13 *"Therefore, brethren, we are debtors—not to the flesh, to live according to the flesh. For if you live according to the flesh you will die; but if by the Spirit you put to death the deeds of the body, you will live."*

This very act also took back Satan's dominion over the nations spiritually and has given Jesus full authority once again over the world. 1 John 3:8 *"The one who does what is sinful is of the devil, because the devil has been sinning from the beginning. The reason the Son of God appeared was to destroy the devil's work."* Before Jesus, we had no out when Satan tempted us, he would always win, but now with Jesus, we can do what James 4:7 *says "and resist the devil by the power of the Holy Spirit living inside of us and Satan must flee."*

Satan no longer has full dominion over the nations and every time that someone gives their life to Jesus, Satan loses his ground. That's why Jesus gave the command in Mathew 28:19 to *"go and make disciples of all the nations, baptizing them in the name of the Father and of the Son and of the Holy Spirit."*

Jesus was claiming ownership and Satan's rule was now over to all those who believe in Him. Jesus is now King of Kings and Lord of Lords. Revelations 19:13,16 *"He is clothed in a robe dipped in blood, and the name by which he is called is The Word of God. . . On His robe and on his thigh, he has a name written, King of kings and Lord of Lords."*

Three Grand Rebellions that Jesus Reversed

Grand Rebellion 1: Adam and Eve sinned and brought death to mankind, but Jesus reversed that curse through His sinless life while He lived on earth and His resurrection, bringing mankind eternal life.

Grand Rebellion 2: The Watchers (Elohim) engaged in sexual sin activity with humans, but Jesus reversed that curse through His virgin birth. By doing so, He brought holiness (Yahweh) to evil and reversed the evil scheme.

Grand Rebellion 3: Nimrod constructed the tower of Babel, which led God to divide humanity based on their inheritance. As a result, mankind was given over to Satan and their sins. However, Jesus reversed the curse by sending the Holy Spirit during Pentecost, allowing representation from all nations to be united once again.

This book has brought to life a more complete Easter story than what many of us have ever known before. Jesus' birth, death, and resurrection overcame an evil attack on mankind. The single thread that runs through the Bible demonstrates that God has never stopped loving and pursuing His creation.

And... His pursuit of man is not yet complete. The book of Acts is still being written, and we have a part to play in reclaiming the territory that Satan had dominion over for all those years.

In the upcoming chapter, we will discover the supernatural power given to us by Jesus, enabling us to accomplish what mankind was unable to do prior to His resurrection.

Chapter 14

Reclaiming Dominion Through Discipleship

Opening Scene:

As the central character in a powerful cinematic scene. Imagine, as dawn breaks, you stand overlooking a vast cityscape, the early light reflecting off buildings that hold stories of millions.

For a moment, all is still, but this stillness is deceptive. For here is a battleground, a place where the invisible wars of everyday life rage on, and each soul is a territory to be won. You are a disciple of Christ, called not only to live out your faith but to act as a beacon, guiding others to the redemptive love of Jesus.

The silence of the dawn is a silent clarion call to you, the disciple, as you absorb the weight of your commission. The city below may still slumber, but you awaken to a deeper reality—a world in desperate need of the Gospel's hope. As the hues of sunrise paint the sky, a breathtaking artwork only the Creator could design, so too are you an artisan of faith, crafted to sow seeds of truth in hearts of stone.

Your hands, once empty, are now tools of transformation; your voice, once uncertain, is a herald of good news. With every stride on these streets, you walk in the footsteps of the apostles, imbued with the Spirit's power to speak life into desolate places. Each person you pass is a narrative unfolding, a life that the love of Christ can rewrite from a tale of despair to a testimony of grace.

You recall the words of 2 Corinthians 5:20, where Paul speaks of being Christ's ambassador—God making His appeal through us. The gravity of these words imprints upon your heart as you ponder the sacred responsibility bestowed upon you. In each encounter, casual or intimate, your life's mission is clear: to replicate the love of the Savior, to imbue each gesture with the fragrance of His presence.

The people of this city, each locked in their own struggles, might seem like an overwhelming harvest, but you remember Jesus' assurance in Luke 10:2—"*The harvest is plentiful, but the laborers are few.*" So, you pray for more laborers, companions in the great co-mission, even as you ready yourself to take up the sword of the Spirit.

You turn back from the skyline and step down into the life of the city, the light now fully cast across the everyday spectrum. Your mission begins anew, each day a fresh opportunity to reclaim lost ground, to disciple one heart at a time, pushing back the darkness with every act of love and every word of truth.

This is the disciple's path, trodden by saints and martyrs before, now given to you—a call to disciple others and to take back land where shadows once fell, making the city on a hill shine all the brighter for His glory.

In Matthew 28:19-20, Jesus commands His followers to *"go and make disciples of all nations."* From the ripple of a single act of obedience can come waves of transformation. As Christ's disciples, we are not just followers; we are commissioned agents of His kingdom, reclaiming land that has been lost to the enemy.

The Mission of Reclamation Through Christ

Narrative:

In the early chapters of Genesis, humanity was entrusted with dominion over the earth (Genesis 1:28). Yet, through sin, this dominion was tarnished, and the enemy, Satan, found his opening.

However, the narrative does not end there. The Bible tells of a Savior, Jesus Christ, who through His life, death, and resurrection, defeated Satan and reclaimed authority (Colossians 2:15). Now, in union with Christ, it falls to us to continue this mission of reclaiming and sanctifying what has been corrupted.

I mentioned at the beginning of this book, I work with an organization called Natural Discipleship. This ministry offers tools to empower even the newest believer in this divine mission of discipleship. The "9 Steps" curriculum of Natural Disciple equips any Christian, regardless of spiritual maturity, to disciple others effectively. This curriculum demystifies the discipleship process, making it an attainable directive for all who wish to see God's kingdom expand.

The journey through discipleship often uncovers areas of life where the enemy has gained a foothold. Natural Discipleship curriculum "Keys to Being Set Free" offers a path toward liberation from such strongholds, addressing hurts, habits, and addictions—territories Satan once claimed. Through sound biblical teaching, this curriculum provides strategies for genuine freedom in Christ, aligning with Galatians 5:1, where we read of the freedom Christ has granted us—a freedom we must stand firm in.

Leadership is at the heart of any spiritual movement, and so our "How to Build a Discipleship Leadership Team" curriculum molds individuals into the image of Christ's leadership style. As Jesus empowered His twelve disciples, entrusting them to build teams of leaders to carry on the work He first started.

Building a leadership team in the context of Christian discipleship is similar to cultivating a garden that, in time, yields an abundant harvest. It starts with the careful selection and nurturing of people who are (FAT) Faith Available and Teachable.

These individuals are committed to discipleship while also living examples of transformative faith. As it's written in Ephesians 4:11-12, *"Christ himself gave the apostles, the prophets, the evangelists, the pastors and teachers, to equip his people for works of service, so that the body of Christ may be built up."*

In this spiritual ecosystem, each leader is both a cultivator and a seed. They grow in their walk with God and, concurrently, sow into the lives of others. As the team strengthens, each person's unique gifts are harnessed to serve and expand the kingdom of God. When functioning effectively, this leadership forms the backbone of a movement, a visible and active expression of God's love and power at work.

In the practical sense, building such a team requires intentionality – equipping leaders through discipleship and practical ministry experience, such as described in 2 Timothy 2:2, where Paul encourages Timothy to entrust the teachings to reliable people who will also be qualified to teach others. Through this process, a multiplicative effect takes place; each leader then disciples others, creating an ever-widening circle of influence.

As momentum builds, this community of leaders can develop into a spiritual movement. Acts 2:46-47 describes the early church's daily growth as they dedicated themselves to fellowship, prayer, and the apostles' teaching. Likewise, your leadership team, through authenticity and shared vision, becomes irresistible to those yearning for spiritual truth and community.

The movement becomes organic and dynamic – a living, breathing entity fueled by the Spirit and characterized by love, service, and transformation. It extends an open invitation, an opportunity for others to join the pathway and be part of something greater than themselves, just as Jesus' disciples did when they dropped their nets and followed Him, leading to a movement that changed the course of history.

This is the pattern of the Kingdom – an expansive, inclusive, and unstoppable force that begins with the heart of discipleship and echoes into eternity.

If you're looking for a good discipleship curriculum that focuses on transformation, both for yourself and for those you'll guide: venture to naturaldiscipleship.com and download the app to ignite the flame of your personal discipleship ministry. The app serves as a gateway to a wealth of resources designed to equip you with the knowledge and skills necessary to foster growth in Christ, reflecting 2 Timothy 2:2.

When choosing whom to disciple, seek those who embody the characteristics of FAT—Faithful, Available, and Teachable. These are the qualities that Jesus sought in His disciples: the faithfulness to follow Him, the availability to dedicate themselves to His mission, and the teachability to embrace His teaching and grow in understanding, as suggested in Luke 9:62 where Jesus speaks about the commitment required to follow Him.

Encourage each of your disciples to replicate this journey, committing to disciple another even as they learn and grow under your guidance. It is through this model of multiplication, reminiscent of the mustard seed parable in Matthew 13:31-32, that the Kingdom of God is propagated—starting from the smallest of beginnings to reach a breadth unfathomable.

This chain of discipleship, where each believer becomes a link to another soul, weaves a strong and expanding network, contributing to the rapid spread of the Gospel.

It transcends the slow pace of addition, bursting forth into multiplication, and reflects God's original intent for His message to flourish across the earth. By embracing the vision of continuous replication, you are stepping into the vital role of a harvester in the Great Commission, contributing to a spiritual renaissance that propels the Kingdom of God forward with unprecedented velocity.

So now we're at the end, but there is still more to come, for every great story in a movie has a beginning and an end. Our story started in the garden, and now our story will end in the next chapter in the new garden.

Chapter 15

The Dawning of Eternity

Opening Scene:

Fade into a scene where you stand upon the precipice of time, gazing out across the twilight of the present age. The world as you know it shimmers and dissolves before your eyes, revealing an eternal dawn.

This is no ordinary daybreak—this is the unveiling of a cosmos reborn, the New Heaven and New Earth prophesied in Revelation 21:1. Like an understudy stepping onto the stage of history, you find yourself at the threshold of an everlasting epilogue where the narrative of humanity finds its fulfillment.

Your heart pulses with the promise of no more death, mourning, crying, or pain, for these former things have passed away (Revelation 21:4). The air is alive with a sacred electricity, a sanctified charge that revives your very soul.

You take your first steps into a world where abundant life has overflowed its banks, inundating creation with the glory of God's unblemished design.

Amidst this celestial landscape, the Tree of Life beckons, its leaves unfurled in a gesture of welcome—a moving echo of the paradise lost now found. The same tree that once graced the Garden of Eden, from which access was once denied, now stands tall by the river of the water of life, clear as crystal, flowing from the throne of God and of the Lamb (Revelation 22:1-2).

It's here, in the New Jerusalem, that Genesis renews its acquaintance with Revelation, the Alpha embraces the Omega, and the story of redemption intertwines with reality.

The presence of the tree signifies a restoration beyond imagination—a healing of the nations and an unbroken fellowship with the Creator. With its fruit yielding every month and leaves for the healing of the nations, the Tree of Life is an emblem of the provision and bounty that characterizes this renewed existence (Revelation 22:2).

In this cinematic picture, Jesus, the Redeemer, walks among us in His eternal city. It is in His light that we see light, His radiance casting no shadow, for there is nothing left to obscure.

The city has no need of sun or moon to shine, for the glory of God gives it light, and the Lamb is its lamp (Revelation 21:23). There will be no night there, no need for lamps or stars, for the Lord God will illuminate all (Revelation 22:5).

As you traverse the streets of transparent gold under an everlasting day, the New Jerusalem unfolds around you in breathtaking splendor. This city, resplendent and radiant, is adorned like a bride for her husband, and Jesus, the Redeemer, is its centerpiece, its reason, its architect.

His presence permeates every corner, every stone, every glimmering facet of the city's expanse. His light is omnipresent, a glow that warms the soul and illuminates the mind (Revelation 21:2, 23).

The air is free from the haze of tears and the shadow of sorrow; the former things have passed away, leaving only purity and joy (Revelation 21:4). As you move, it's as though you're walking through liquid light: it's tangible and enfolds you, a reminder that you are now part of a reality that far surpasses the transient shades of the old world.

In this sacred metropolis, peace is not merely an absence of conflict—it is a tangible presence, emanating from Jesus Himself, "the Prince of Peace" (Isaiah 9:6). His light does more than dispel darkness; it is a beacon of unfathomable love, an eternal testament to the grace that has led you down the path to your eternal home in the eternal city.

In Jesus's light, we find not just the illumination of our surroundings but the revelation of God's truth. Here, we understand fully as we have been fully understood. The mysteries of faith, once enshrouded in human limitation, are now laid bare, resplendent in the light of the Lamb (1 Corinthians 13:12).

Around the throne of God, a river pulses with life, a crystal-clear torrent that nourishes and refreshes. Alongside its banks sprawls the Tree of Life, its leaves a canopy of renewal for the people drawn from every tongue and nation. Its branches are extended invitations, a call to partake in the everlasting fruit, each serving as a monthly reminder of God's ceaseless provision (Revelation 22:2).

In this everlasting light, there is no need for temples or sanctuaries, for the Almighty and the Lamb are the temple (Revelation 21:22). Their presence is the sacred space, an infinite expanse where worship occurs with every beat of the glorified heart.

This is the destination of every longing, the conclusion of every pilgrim journey: to dwell in the presence of Jesus, where the radiance of God rests upon us for all eternity. The divine and humankind are once again in fellowship as God's original plan is now complete.

As the curtains draw to a close on this cinematic journey, we find ourselves at the finale—the culmination of God's grand plan. The narrative has reached its crowning point, guiding us to the very destination that has been preordained since time's dawn.

Here, in this moment of sacred realization, we stand where divine foresight has always meant for us to stand, encompassed by the fulfillment of a purpose set forth from the beginning. This is the place of intended convergence, where God's plan and our paths intersect, marking not an end, but the commencement of an eternal communion with the Creator.

Our life's story is written by God himself and He portrays a love for us that we could never have earned. He is worthy of our admiration, and I hope this book motivates you to persevere. Keep pursuing Jesus with an unwavering enthusiasm. Never surrender, remain resilient, and finish strong. May we go together and make disciples until He calls us home. May God richly bless you and your family and your family's family.

Resources / References

Chapter 1:

1. https://www.thedivinecouncil.com/

Chapter 3:

1. https://drmsh.com/divine-council/
2. https://www.christiancentury.org/article/interview/
   jesus-second-temple-era-jew
3. https://www.gatewaysofhislight.com/bookofenoch/
   enochisauthoritative/

Chapter 6:

1. https://www.gotquestions.org/consequences-of-
   sin.html

Chapter 9:

1. https://literarydevices.net/the-watchers-in-the-bible/

Chapter 10:

1. "The Book of Enoch" - This ancient Jewish text provides in-depth information about the Nephilim and their involvement in the events surrounding the flood. It offers insights into their survival and transformation.
2. "The Mythology of the Nephilim" by Brian Godawa - In this book, the author explores the myths and theories surrounding the Nephilim, their survival, and their potential role in the development of demonic entities.
3. "Biblical Giants: The Philistines and the Nephilim" by Jean-Jacques Rowe - This work delves into the biblical accounts of giants, including the Nephilim, and explores possible connections to other ancient Near Eastern myths
4. https://creation.com/giant-goliath-evidences

Chapter 11:

1. https://www.miqlat.org/the-tower-of-babel-and-holy-ground-video.htm

EXTRA Resources:

1. Michael S. Heiser "The Unseen Realm: Recovering the Supernatural Worldview of the Bible" (2019). He examines the ancient context of Scripture, explaining how its supernatural worldview can help us grow in our understanding of God. He illuminates intriguing and amazing passages of the Bible that have been hiding in plain sight. You'll find yourself engaged in an enthusiastic pursuit of the truth, resulting in a new appreciation for God's Word.

2. Amar Annus, "On the Origin of the Watchers: A Comparative Study of the Antediluvian Wisdom in Mesopotamian and Jewish Traditions," Journal for the Study of the Pseudepigrapha 19.4 (2010): 277–320

3. James C. Vanderkam and George W. E. Nickelsburg, 1 Enoch: The Hermeneia Translation (Fortress Press, 2012)

4. James C. VanderKam, "1 Enoch, Enochic Motifs, and Enoch in Early Christian Literature," in The Jewish Apocalyptic Heritage in Early Christianity; ed. James C. VanderKam and William Adler; Minneapolis: Fortress, 1996), 33–101

5. Archie T. Wright, The Origin of Evil Spirits: The Reception of Genesis 6:1-4 in Early Jewish Literature, Revised Edition (Wissenschaftliche Untersuchungen zum Neuen Testament 198, second series; Tübingen: Mohr Siebeck, 2013)

6. Annette Yoshiko Reed, Fallen Angels and the History of Judaism and Christianity: The Reception of

Enochic Literature (Cambridge: Cambridge University Press, 2005)

7. James C. Vanderkam and George W. E. Nickelsburg, 1 Enoch: The Hermeneia Translation (Fortress Press, 2012)
8. Benjamin Foster, Before The Muses: An Anthology Of Akkadian Literature
9. Benjamin Foster, From Distant Days: Myths, Tales, and Poetry of Ancient Mesopotamia
10. John Walton, The Lost World of Genesis One: Ancient Cosmology and the Origins Debate
11. John Walton, Ancient Israelite Literature in its Cultural Context
12. John Walton, The Lost World of Scripture: Ancient Literary Culture and Biblical Authority
13. John Walton, Genesis 1 as Ancient Cosmology

Keys to being Set Free

Overcoming Hang-ups, Hurts & Addictions

Are you tired of being held captive by hurts, addictions, and hang-ups?

Has your spiritual journey become stagnant and nearly devoid of vitality?

Do you yearn for a life of genuine freedom, where the burden of your current lifestyle no longer determines your current state? Look no further. Keys to Being Set Free is a one-on-one transformative discipleship curriculum you've been looking for.

In this life-changing book, you will embark on a journey guided by biblically balanced principles and practical wisdom. This journey will help addresses the hurts, addictions, and hang-ups that can hinder your spiritual growth and your intimate relationship with the Father. You will discover the keys that will unlock the door to lasting change and restoration.

Order your copy today online at:

Conquer Through Surrender

A Survival Guide to Overcoming Life's Toughest Trials

Life is full of challenges, and as Christians, we often struggle to navigate through life's difficulties. Our trials can sometimes overwhelm us, making our lives take unexpected and undesired turns. In our search for answers, we cry out to God for help, often feeling as if He isn't listening.

Perhaps you've sought God in the past but haven't experienced the goodness others speak of, encountering only pain instead.

This book is designed to help followers of Christ learn to thrive amid their circumstances. It teaches you how to find joy even in life's hardest moments. This is a book you'll return to time and again, finding answers to your questions and renewed hope for tomorrow. Ultimately, you will discover God's perspective and understand just how much He loves you and desires to bless you.

Learn How to Thrive Spiritually in Every Moment

Order your copy today online at:

BARNES&NOBLE
BOOKSELLERS

www.ingramcontent.com/pod-product-compliance
Lightning Source LLC
Chambersburg PA
CBHW050748150726
48196CB00004B/381